At Sylvan, we believe reading is one of life's most important, most personal, most meaningful skills, and we're so glad you've taken this step to build strong reading skills with us. Reading comprehension is the foundation of success in all aspects of fourth-grade academics and beyond. As a successful reader, you hold infinite possibilities in your hands, enabling you to learn about anything and everything. That's because the more you read, the more you learn. And the more you learn, the more connections you can make to the world around you.

At Sylvan, successful reading instruction encompasses numerous reading acquisition processes with research-based, developmentally appropriate, and highly motivating, entertaining, and thought-provoking lessons. The learning process relies on high standards and meaningful parental involvement. With success, students feel increasing confidence. With increasing confidence, students build even more success. It's a perfect cycle. That's why our Sylvan workbooks aren't like the others. We're laying out the roadmap for learning. The rest is in your hands.

Parents, you have a special role. While your child is working, stay within earshot. If he needs help or gets stuck, you can be there to get him on the right track. And you're always there with supportive encouragement and plenty of celebratory congratulations.

One of the best ways to see learning progress is to check one's own work. Each section of the workbook includes a Check It! strip. As your child completes the activities, he can check his answers with Check It! If he sees any errors, he can fix them himself.

Included with your purchase is a coupon for a discount on our in-center service. As your child continues on his academic journey, your local Sylvan Learning Center can partner with your family in ensuring your child remains a confident, successful, and independent learner.

The Sylvan Team

D1520256

Sylvan Learning Center.
Unleash your child's potential here.

No matter how big or small the academic challenge, every child has the ability to learn. But sometimes children need help making it happen. Sylvan believes every child has the potential to do great things. And, we know better than anyone else how to tap into that academic potential so that a child's future really is full of possibilities. Sylvan Learning Center is the place where your child can build and master the learning skills needed to succeed and unlock the potential you know is there.

The proven, personalized approach of our in-center programs deliver unparalleled results that other supplemental education services simply can't match. Your child's achievements will be seen not only in test scores and report cards but outside the classroom as well. And when he starts achieving his full potential, everyone will know it. You will see a new level of confidence come through in everything he does and every interaction he has.

How can Sylvan's personalized in-center approach help your child unleash his potential?

• Starting with our exclusive Sylvan Skills Assessment®, we pinpoint your child's exact academic needs.

• Then we develop a customized learning plan designed to achieve your child's academic goals.

• Through our method of skill mastery, your child will not only learn and master every skill in his personalized plan, he will be truly motivated and inspired to achieve his full potential.

To get started, included with this Sylvan product purchase is $10 off our exclusive Sylvan Skills Assessment®. Simply use this coupon and contact your local Sylvan Learning Center to set up your appointment.

And to learn more about Sylvan and our innovative in-center programs, call 1-800-EDUCATE or visit www.educate.com. *With over 1,100 locations in North America, there is a Sylvan Learning Center near you!*

4th-Grade Reading Comprehension Success

Copyright © 2009 by Sylvan Learning, Inc.

Published in the United States by Random House, Inc., New York, and in Canada by Random House of Canada Limited, Toronto.

www.tutoring.sylvanlearning.com

Created by Smarterville Productions LLC
Cover and Interior Photos: Jonathan Pozniak
Cover and Interior Illustrations: Duendes del Sur

First Edition

ISBN: 978-0-375-43003-9

Library of Congress Cataloging-in-Publication Data available upon request.

This book is available at special discounts for bulk purchases for sales promotions or premiums. For more information, write to Special Markets/Premium Sales, 1745 Broadway, MD 6-2, New York, New York 10019 or e-mail specialmarkets@randomhouse.com.

PRINTED IN CHINA

10 9 8 7 6 5 4 3 2

Contents

Checking your answers is part of the learning.

Each section of the workbook begins with an easy-to-use Check It! strip.

1. Before beginning the activities, cut out the Check It! strip.

2. As you complete the activities on each page, check your answers.

3. If you find an error, you can correct it yourself.

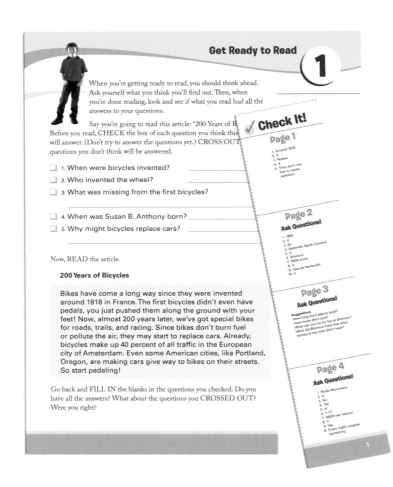

1

When you're getting ready to read, you should think ahead. Ask yourself what you think you'll find out. Then, when you're done reading, look and see if what you read had all the answers to your questions.

Say you're going to read this article: "200 Years of Bicycles." Before you read, CHECK the box of each question you think this article will answer. (Don't try to answer the questions yet.) CROSS OUT the questions you don't think will be answered.

☐ 1. When were bicycles invented? _____

☐ 2. Who invented the wheel? _____

☐ 3. What was missing from the first bicycles?

_____

☐ 4. When was Susan B. Anthony born? _____

☐ 5. Why might bicycles replace cars? _____

_____

Now, READ the article.

200 Years of Bicycles

Bikes have come a long way since they were invented around 1818 in France. The first bicycles didn't even have pedals, you just pushed them along the ground with your feet! Now, almost 200 years later, we've got special bikes for roads, trails, and racing. Since bikes don't burn fuel or pollute the air, they may start to replace cars. Already, bicycles make up 40 percent of all traffic in the European city of Amsterdam. Even some American cities, like Portland, Oregon, are making cars give way to bikes on their streets. So start pedaling!

Go back and FILL IN the blanks in the questions you checked. Do you have all the answers? What about the questions you crossed out? Were you right?

✓ Check It!

Page 1

1. Around 1818.
2. X
3. Pedals.
4. X
5. They don't use fuel or cause pollution.

Page 2
Ask Questions!

1. 1895
2. X
3. 43
4. Asheville, North Carolina
5. X
6. Biltmore
7. 8000 acres
8. X
9. George Vanderbilt
10. X

Page 3
Ask Questions!

Suggestions:
-How long did it take to build?
-How much did it cost?
-What can you do for fun at Biltmore?
-What did Biltmore have that other homes of the time didn't have?

Page 4
Ask Questions!

1. Rocky Mountains
2. X
3. No
4. 150
5. X
6. 7–17
7. $3000 per session
8. X
9. Yes
10. Every night, weather permitting

✓ Check It!

Page 6

Ask Questions!

Suggestions:
-What can you do on Lake MacShane?
-What sports tournaments are there?
-What does "Kimimela" mean?
-Are boys allowed at Camp Kimimela?
-About how many campers are there?
-What are the cabins like?

Page 7

Ask Questions!

Possible Questions:
-What is the nose made out of?
-What is inside my nose?
-Why do we have snot?
-Why do we sneeze?
-How do we smell things?

Page 8

Ask Questions!

Did the article answer all of
your questions?

Ask Questions!

Say you're going to read this article: "The Biggest Home in America."

Before you read, CHECK the box of each question you think this article will answer. CROSS OUT the questions you don't think will be answered.

☐ 1. When was the biggest home built?

☐ 2. What is the capital of Kentucky?

☐ 3. How many bathrooms does the biggest home have?

☐ 4. Where is the biggest home in America?

☐ 5. Did Ben Franklin really discover electricity?

☐ 6. What is the biggest home called?

☐ 7. How big is the backyard of the biggest home?

☐ 8. Why can't penguins fly?

☐ 9. Who built the biggest home?

☐ 10. Is there a law that says kids can't stay up all night?

Now, READ the article.

The Biggest Home in America

Would you like to live in the biggest home in America? Then head down to Asheville, North Carolina. That's where you'll find Biltmore—a palace built by millionaire George Vanderbilt in 1895. Don't forget to pack your swing set— Biltmore's backyard covers 8000 acres! And you'll need lots of toilet paper for the 43 bathrooms. There's also an indoor pool and bowling alley, just in case you get bored. The house took more than six years to build. No one's sure how much it cost, but consider this: it had electric lights, indoor bathrooms, central heating, and an elevator during a time when most people were still using outhouses and oil lamps!

Go back and FILL IN the blanks in the questions you checked. Do you have all the answers?

WRITE down three more questions that this article answers.

_____

_____

_____

_____

_____

Ask Questions!

Are you looking for a sleep-away camp? Read this brochure: "Be a Butterfly!"

Before you read, CHECK the box of each question you think this brochure will answer. CROSS OUT the questions you don't think will be answered.

1. ☐ Where is Camp Kimimela? _____

2. ☐ Are other camps better than Camp Kimimela? _____

3. ☐ Can I bring a cell phone to Camp Kimimela? _____

4. ☐ How many acres does Camp Kimimela cover? _____

5. ☐ Do lots of campers get homesick and leave Camp Kimimela? _____

6. ☐ How old are the campers? _____

7. ☐ How much does going to the camp cost? _____

8. ☐ How many kids have been injured at Camp Kimimela? _____

9. ☐ Can I play tennis and volleyball at Camp Kimimela? _____

10. ☐ When do they have campfires at Camp Kimimela? _____

Now, READ the brochure.

Be a Butterfly!

Camp Kimimela is a camp for girls in the beautiful Rocky Mountains. *Kimimela* means "butterfly" in the Native American Sioux language. Our campers stay in cabins named after different butterflies: Lacewings (ages 7–10), Swallowtails (ages 11–14), and Monarchs (15–17). While here, campers will live, play, and learn under the careful watch of a team of trained counselors.

Our camp is on 150 acres that include woods and a lake.

Camp activities include boating and swimming on beautiful Lake MacShane, as well as horseback riding and hiking in the woods. Campers may also join in sports tournaments (tennis, archery, and volleyball) and cabin skits and parties. Every day ends with a "Snack & Sing" around the campfire (weather permitting).

Our ten cozy cabins hold about 15 campers each. Don't worry—the cabins all have bunk beds, electricity, and bathrooms!

Since Camp Kimimela is all about outdoor fun, you may not bring cell phones, MP3 players, or hand-held game systems. Parent phone calls are limited to one per week.

Our six-week sessions run from June to mid-July and mid-July through August. The cost is $3000 per session for one child. The deadline for applications is May 1st.

If you have any questions, please contact our management office.

GO BACK and FILL IN the blanks in the questions you checked. Do you have all the answers? WRITE down five more questions that this article answers.

_____

_____

_____

_____

_____

Ask Questions!

Curious about your sniffer? Read the article on the following page: "Your Nose: Inside and Out."
Before you read, WRITE some questions you think this article will answer. There's extra room so you
can come back after you read and fill in the answers.

1. Question: _____

_____

_____

_____

2. Question: _____

_____

_____

_____

3. Question: _____

_____

_____

_____

4. Question: _____

_____

_____

_____

Now, READ the article.

Your Nose: Inside and Out

Noses come in all shapes and sizes. The part that sticks out of your face isn't bone—it's mostly *cartilage*, a kind of tissue that is strong, but wobbly.

Men have longer noses than women, but women have a better sense of smell!

When we breathe through our noses, we suck in way more than just air. That's why we need hair and snot in our noses! Snot (also called *mucus*) is made out of water, salt, and other chemicals so it's thick and sticky. The hair blocks the dust, pollen, and other bad junk from getting into your lungs. Then the snot sticks to it and pulls it down into your stomach when you sniff and swallow. Or, you can blow the bad junk out of your nose, along with the snot.

A strong sneeze can shoot snot out of your nose at over 100 miles per hour!

What about smell? Odor molecules are very light, and they float up through your nose to the very back. That's where you've got a bunch of nerves that catch odors and report them to your brain.

Your sense of smell goes hand in hand with your sense of taste. If something smells rotten, you probably won't eat it because your nose knows it will make you sick! Thanks, Sniffie!

GO BACK and look at the questions you asked. ANSWER them. ADD any new questions and the answers you learned here.

_____

_____

_____

 **Check It!**

Cut out the Check It! section on page 1, and see if you got the answers right.

Another question to ask yourself before reading is "What do I already know?" Then, when you're done reading, you can ask: "What did I learn?" Try it out!

First, READ the topic. Then FILL IN the What Do I Already Know? column. After that, you'll be ready to read!

Topic: Tomatoes

What Do I Already Know?

_____

_____

_____

_____

_____

_____

_____

What Did I Learn?

_____

_____

_____

_____

_____

_____

There's Nothing Rotten about Tomatoes!

We all know that tomatoes are good for us. But did you know that tomatoes are actually fruit? That's right! Tomatoes contain seeds and grow from a flowering plant—just like a strawberry. But since the tomato isn't sweet, it's generally considered a vegetable. Here's another fact about tomatoes: Every August, a town in Spain hosts *La Tomatina*, a massive food fight using tons of rotten tomatoes. Sounds like fun—as long as you don't have to clean up afterward!

Time to GO BACK and FILL IN the What Did I Learn? column. CROSS OUT any facts in the first column you got wrong. See how this works?

✓ Check It!

Page 9

Suggestions:
 Know:
  1. Tomato is red.
  2. Tomato is a veggie.
  3. Tomato is good for you.
  4. You make ketchup out of tomatoes.

 Learned:
  1. Tomatoes are fruit.
  2. Fruits contain seeds and grow from flowering plants.
  3. A town in Spain has a tomato fight every year.

Page 10

Suggestions:
 Know:
  1. There are nine planets.
  2. The planets revolve around the sun.
  3. Jupiter is the biggest planet.
  4. Saturn has rings.

 Learned:
  1. Pluto is not a planet.
  2. The sun is the largest object in the solar system.
  3. The system also includes moons, comets, and asteroids.
  4. There are three asteroids in close orbit to Earth.
  5. There's an asteroid belt.

Page 12

Suggestions:
 Know:
  1. Spiders are bugs.
  2. Spiders are deadly.
  3. Spiders spin webs.
  4. The tarantula is big and hairy.

 Learned:
  1. Spiders aren't insects.
  2. Spiders are carnivores.
  3. Few spiders actually hurt humans.
  4. The tarantula can kill with its hair.
  5. Some spiders hunt without webs.

✓ Check It!

Page 14

Suggestions:

Know:
1. Fairies aren't real.
2. I know about the tooth fairy.
3. Fairies have magic.
4. I've read about fairies in stories.

Learned:
1. There are lots of fairies in fiction.
2. People used to really believe in fairies.
3. *Brownies* and *pookahs* are kinds of fairies.
4. People used iron to ward off fairies.
5. There is a legend behind the tooth fairy.
6. Two girls took fake fairy photos in 1917.

Before & After Questions

FILL IN the What Do I Already Know? column.

Topic: The Solar System

What Do I Already Know?	What Did I Learn?
_____	_____
_____	_____
_____	_____
_____	_____
_____	_____
_____	_____
_____	_____
_____	_____
_____	_____
_____	_____
_____	_____
_____	_____
_____	_____
_____	_____
_____	_____
_____	_____
_____	_____

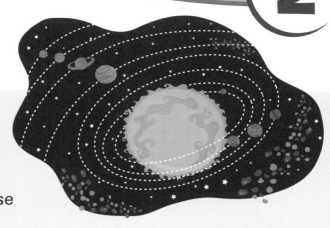

Now, READ the article.

Our Corner of the Universe

The solar system is nine planets and the sun, right? WRONG. There's a lot more going on in our little corner of the universe than you think.

First of all, there are only eight planets. Sorry, Pluto, but experts have decided that you're not really a planet. (That's okay, Earth still loves you!)

So the planets of the solar system are: Mercury (closest to the sun), then Venus, Earth, Mars, Jupiter, Saturn, and Neptune.

Pluto used to come last in the lineup. But now it's considered a *dwarf planet*, which means that it's not really big enough to count as a planet. Other dwarf planets are Ceres and Eris.

There's more to the solar system than just the planets. The sun, of course, is the largest object in the solar system. But the system also includes moons, comets, and asteroids.

Scientists have learned a lot about the biggest asteroids. There are three that have orbits close to Earth: Atens, Apollos, and Amors. There's also a huge *asteroid belt* between Mars and Jupiter. This "belt" is like a highway for lots of asteroids.

It may sound like the solar system is a crowded place. Not! There are millions (sometimes billions) of miles between the planets and asteroids. They don't call it "space" for nothing!

Did you learn anything? GO BACK and FILL IN the What Did I Learn? column.

Before & After Questions

FILL IN the What Do I Already Know? column.

Topic: Spiders

What Do I Already Know?

_____

_____

_____

_____

_____

_____

_____

_____

_____

_____

_____

_____

What Did I Learn?

_____

_____

_____

_____

_____

_____

_____

_____

_____

_____

_____

_____

Now, READ the article.

Tiny Hunters: Spiders

Spiders are really interesting creatures, but they're not insects. Nope! Spiders are arachnids. Unlike insects, arachnids have eight (or more) legs, and they don't have antennae or wings. Other famous arachnids include scorpions and ticks. Spiders are *carnivores*, which means that they eat other living creatures.

All spiders can spin webs. Some spiders use webs to catch insects. But other spiders actually hunt their prey, just like tiny lions. A large tarantula can chase down and kill a small lizard or a bird!

The tarantula is probably the scariest spider. It can grow as big as 4 inches, with 12-inch legs. But tarantulas hardly ever bite, and they're generally harmless. People even keep them as pets! Strange fact: Some tarantulas have sharp, poisonous body hair that they throw at attackers. The poison on these hairs can kill a small mouse.

Most spiders bite, though, and use poison to protect themselves or kill their prey. But very few kinds of spiders can hurt humans. In all of North America, there are only five or six really harmful kinds, including the black widow and the brown recluse. Still, any time you get a spider bite, you should get it checked out!

Did you learn anything? GO BACK and FILL IN the What Did I Learn? column.

Before & After Questions

FILL IN the What Do I Already Know? column.

Topic: Fairies

What Do I Already Know?

_____

_____

_____

_____

_____

_____

_____

_____

_____

_____

_____

_____

_____

_____

What Did I Learn?

_____

_____

_____

_____

_____

_____

_____

_____

_____

_____

_____

_____

_____

_____

Now, READ the article.

Fairies: Fact & Fiction

There are lots of famous fairies in fiction. Where would Cinderella be without her fairy godmother? Or Peter Pan without Tinkerbell? Narnia is filled with fairies! Even more recent books, like *Artemis Fowl* and the *Spiderwick Chronicles*, are about people who try to learn all the secrets of the fairy world.

For hundreds of years, many people really believed in fairies. They blamed fairies for strange weather, natural wonders, or sudden illness. They thought naughty fairies like *brownies* and *pookahs* would steal objects or damage crops. Some thought bad fairies would take human babies and replace them with fairy babies (called *changelings*). They even blamed fairies when they got lost in the woods!

To get rid of fairies, people used iron, four-leaf clovers, or even bread. But not everybody disliked fairies. People who wanted to attract fairies built little houses for them to live in!

TURN the page to keep reading!

The most famous fairy story is, of course, about the tooth fairy. In the old days, some people believed that baby teeth were really powerful. They thought if a mean fairy took the teeth, she could work evil magic on the children. So, parents would bury their kids' teeth to keep them safe. Later, this practice changed to "burying" the tooth under a pillow or in a glass of water by the bed. Then, people thought the tooth fairy (a good fairy) would come and replace the tooth with money or a gift. This is a much nicer legend!

In 1917, two young girls took photographs of fairies flying around their backyard in Cottingley, England. The photos looked so real that people believed they were proof that fairies existed. Even the author of the *Sherlock Holmes* books, Sir Arthur Conan Doyle, was a believer! Years later, one of the girls confessed that all the pictures were fakes. The "fairies" were really cut out of paper. But in 2001, their photos sold for over $12,000!

There will always be people who want to believe in fairies. How about you?

Did you learn anything? GO BACK and FILL IN the What Did I Learn? column.

Check It!

Cut out the Check It! section on page 9, and see if you got the answers right.

Get Ready to Read

PICK a new nonfiction book or article to read today. Before you start reading, FILL OUT this worksheet.

The title is _____

The topic is _____

_____

I think it will answer these questions _____

_____

_____

_____

_____

_____

_____

_____

When you're done reading, CHECK all the questions that were answered. CROSS OUT the questions that weren't answered.

What other questions did it answer? _____

_____

_____

_____

_____

_____

Get Ready to Read

PICK a new nonfiction book or article to read today. Before you start reading, FILL OUT this worksheet.

The title is _____

The topic is _____

_____

I think it will answer these questions _____

_____

_____

_____

_____

_____

When you're done reading, CHECK all the questions that were answered. CROSS OUT the questions that weren't answered.

What other questions did it answer? _____

_____

_____

_____

_____

_____

What Do You Know?

PICK a new nonfiction book or article to read today. Before you start reading, FILL OUT this worksheet.

The title is _____

Before you begin to read:

1. LOOK at the book cover or front page of the article.

2. SKIM through the story.

3. ASK yourself what you know about the subject.

What do I know?

1. _____

2. _____

3. _____

4. _____

5. _____

What did I learn?

1. _____

2. _____

3. _____

4. _____

5. _____

What Do You Know?

PICK a new nonfiction book or article to read today. Before you start, FILL OUT this worksheet.

The title is _____

Before you begin to read:

1. LOOK at the book cover or front page of the article.

2. SKIM through the story.

3. ASK yourself what you know about the subject.

What do I know?

1. _____

2. _____

3. _____

4. _____

5. _____

What did I learn?

1. _____

2. _____

3. _____

4. _____

5. _____

Sometimes authors are tricky. They like to write about things without actually telling you what those things are. Why? Because it makes you curious. It makes you read between the lines!

READ this story.

Timmy and the Truck

Timmy had lived at 328 Hampton Drive ever since he was little. It was an exciting place! Every now and then, a loud bell would ring, and all the men would drop what they were doing, slide down a pole, and jump on a big red truck. Then the truck would race out of the garage, lights blazing and siren screaming. Timmy wished he could ride the truck too. But he was always there when the truck came back, wagging his tail and barking "Hello!"

Now, CHECK the right answers, and FILL IN the blanks.

1. What's at 328 Hampton Drive?
   - ☐ a. A dance club
   - ☐ b. A Chinese restaurant
   - ☐ c. A firehouse

How do you know?

_____

2. Who is Timmy?
   - ☐ a. A fireman
   - ☐ b. A little boy
   - ☐ c. A fire dog

How do you know?

_____

See? You're too smart to let an author trick you. Let's do some more!

☑ **Check It!**

Page 21

1. c: fire bell, fire pole, big red truck
2. c: wags tail and barks

Page 22
Check, Please!

1. c: same mom, Ophelia is two minutes older
2. a: front seat, pedaling, "backseat biker"

Page 23
Check, Please!

1. a: kids are dancing, yummy food
2. c: Zella is Red Riding Hood, Evan's a clown, Tory's a vampire
3. b: people moo at Amit and ask him for milk

Pages 24-25
Check, Please!

1. c: face is pale, hands are shaking
2. b: corset, hoop skirts, President Lincoln
3. a: "joined up," fighting rebels, he's on Lincoln's side
4. c: Helena stepped out the front door then sat down.
5. b: work in her lap, wool, needles

✓ **Check It!**

Pages 26-28

Author! Author!

Ask a friend to read your stories
to try to read between the lines!

Check, Please!

READ this story.

> **On the Go**
>
> "I want to ride in front!" yelled Ophelia.
> "Too bad," said Felix. "I got on first."
> "But I'm the oldest."
> "Only by, like, two minutes. Get over it and start pedaling!"
> "Where are we going?" asked Ophelia.
> "To see Mom at her office," said Felix.
> "That's like three miles! We'll never make it!"
> "You're out of shape."
> "Watch out! You almost hit that cat."
> "Stop being a backseat biker!"

Now, CHECK the right answers, and FILL IN the blanks.

1. Who are Ophelia and Felix?

   ☐ a. Best friends

   ☐ b. Worst enemies

   ☐ c. Twins

   How do you know?

   _____

2. What are they doing?

   ☐ a. Riding a bicycle built for two

   ☐ b. Driving a car

   ☐ c. Riding their bikes

   How do you know?

   _____

Check, Please!

READ this story.

Moo!

Everyone was having a great time, except for Amit. Sure, there was yummy food, and some kids were dancing, but Amit was mad. His friend Zella looked great in her red riding hood, and Evan made a funny-looking clown. This only made Amit madder.

"What's wrong, Amit?" asked Tory, who was a vampire. "Aren't you having fun?"

"If one more person moos at me, or asks if I 'got milk,' I'm leaving!"

Tory laughed. "Poor Amit! Maybe you should have worn something else."

Now, CHECK the right answers, and FILL IN the blanks.

1. Where is Amit?

☐ a. At a party ☐ b. In school ☐ c. Selling candy door-to-door

How do you know?

_____

2. What kind of party is it?

☐ a. A birthday party ☐ b. A slumber party ☐ c. A costume party

How do you know?

_____

3. What is Amit wearing?

☐ a. A space suit ☐ b. A cow costume ☐ c. A wizard's hat

How do you know?

_____

Check, Please!

READ this story.

Wally at War

It was a hot day, and Helena's corset was tight around her rib cage as she washed the dishes.

"Helena!" called Mama. "Come out here for a minute."

"Yes'm," Helena said. She stepped out the front door and dropped into a chair, arranging the hoops under her skirts so that they didn't stick up.

"Mr. Birdsley came by," said Mama. Her face was pale and her work was lying in her lap. "He says there's a big battle going on over in Gettysburg, Pennsylvania."

Helena gasped. "Pennsylvania! But that's where Wally's last letter came from! Do you think...?"

Mama's hands were shaking as she picked up a ball of wool that had fallen. "I told that boy not to join up and fight those rotten rebels!"

"He's trying to keep this country together, Mama," said Helena. "Mr. Lincoln says—"

"I don't care what the President says!" Mama snapped. Suddenly, she burst into tears, and her long needles fell to the floor with a clack.

Now, CHECK the right answers, and FILL IN the blanks.

1. Why is Mama crying?

☐ a. She's angry at Helena.

☐ b. She's angry at Wally.

☐ c. She's afraid for Wally.

How do you know?

_____

2. When does this scene take place?

- ❏ a. In the future
- ❏ b. In the past
- ❏ c. Present day

How do you know?

_____

3. Who is Wally?

- ❏ a. A soldier fighting in a war
- ❏ b. A farmer
- ❏ c. A newspaper reporter

How do you know?

_____

4. Where are Mama and Helena sitting?

- ❏ a. In the kitchen
- ❏ b. At church
- ❏ c. On the front porch

How do you know?

_____

5. What was Mama doing?

- ❏ a. Working on a crossword puzzle
- ❏ b. Knitting
- ❏ c. Shelling peas

How do you know?

_____

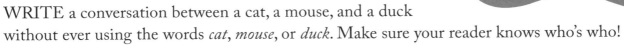

Author! Author!

Now it's YOUR turn!

WRITE a conversation between a cat, a mouse, and a duck
without ever using the words *cat*, *mouse*, or *duck*. Make sure your reader knows who's who!

HINT: How would a cat talk to a mouse? Would a duck have a funny voice? What would their names
be? What do they look like?

_____

_____

_____

_____

_____

_____

_____

_____

_____

_____

_____

_____

_____

_____

_____

_____

_____

_____

Author! Author!

WRITE about an argument between best friends about their favorite TV shows. And get this: the kids are in a cave on a camping trip. But don't say they're in a cave, and don't use the words *TV* or *television*.

HINT: What are the names of the TV shows? What do the kids like about them? What do you find in caves? Bats? Stalactites? How would their voices sound in a cave?

_____

_____

_____

_____

_____

_____

_____

_____

_____

_____

_____

_____

_____

_____

_____

_____

Author! Author!

WRITE about a kid playing checkers with his dad on a sailboat in the ocean. Don't say that they're on a sailboat. Don't use the word *checkers*.

HINT: You can say "King me!" or "I'll be red." You can talk about the parts of the sailboat, or how it's rocking on the ocean. Describe the ocean too!

_____

_____

_____

_____

_____

_____

_____

_____

_____

_____

_____

_____

_____

_____

✓ Check It!

Cut out the Check It! section on page 21, and see if you got the answers right.

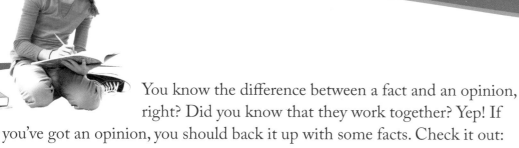

You know the difference between a fact and an opinion, right? Did you know that they work together? Yep! If you've got an opinion, you should back it up with some facts. Check it out:

Question: Should kids have cell phones?

FILL IN some more facts to support each opinion.

OPINION	FACTS
YES	Kids can call parents in an emergency.
YES	Home phone lines aren't tied up.
YES	Kids can be more independent.
YES	_____
YES	_____
YES	_____
NO	Kids will use the phone too much.
NO	Phones and minutes are expensive.
NO	Kids could lose the phone or have it stolen.
NO	_____
NO	_____
NO	_____

Any time a news story or nonfiction article states an opinion, you should always look for the facts. Then you can make up your OWN mind!

✓ Check It!

Page 29

Suggestions:
YES:
1. Phones are cool.
2. Kids need to learn to use this essential gadget.
3. Kids can learn about managing money from the monthly bill.

NO:
1. Phones keep kids from socializing in person.
2. Phones keep kids from playing outside or exercising.
3. Phones in school or at the dinner table are bad manners.

Page 31

Suggestions:
YES:
1. Skaters can teach each other tricks.
2. Skaters could have a tournament.
3. Pietown could become famous for skateboarding.

NO:
1. It's not safe for kids who don't skate well.
2. Skater kids may misbehave.
3. It'll cost $5 to get in.

Page 33

Suggestions:
YES:
1. Next-door neighbors.
2. Thalia comes when Sabeena needs her.
3. Thalia knows how to cheer Sabeena up.
4. Families are best friends too.

NO:
1. Thalia borrows stuff and doesn't give it back.
2. Thalia tells lies about Sabeena to other kids.
3. Thalia is a bad sport.
4. Thalia is a hair-puller.

Page 36

Fact & Opinion

Suggestions:
YES:
1. Zoos have been around since 1793.
2. Animals are cared for in zoos: fed, safe, and healthy.
3. Scientists and the public learn a lot from animals in zoos.
4. Families can't see many animals in the wild.
5. Zoos breed endangered animals.

Continued on the back

Check It!

Page 36

Suggestions:
NO:
1. Animals aren't comfortable: there's no space.
2. Animals aren't behaving naturally in zoos.
3. Animals develop strange behaviors in zoos.
4. It's better to save the natural habitats of wild animals, because that helps the planet.
5. Only a few species have survived being born in captivity.

Q: Should Pieville open a skate park?

First, READ the news story.

New Skate Park on Mozzarella Street

Pietown is buzzing about Mayor Bixby Stiggle's plan to build a skate park next to the library.

"Pietown supports young athletes," said the mayor. "We provide basketball courts and baseball diamonds. A skate park is a logical next step."

"Why should those skater kids get a park? This town needs a good playground for toddlers first!" said Eva T. Finkle, who lives near the library.

Donald Sabin is pleased about the plan, but worried: "If it keeps skaters out of the empty pools in town, that's great. But is it safe for kids who don't skate well? And some of those skater kids are bad news. Will there be a grownup making sure everyone behaves?"

But his son DJ can't wait to try it out: "It'll be great to have a place just for skaters. It's a chance for us to get together and teach each other tricks. Maybe we can even have a tournament. Pietown could be famous for skateboarding!"

There is one thing that DJ doesn't like, though: The town will probably charge skaters $5 to enter the park.

Now, FILL IN the facts.

OPINION	FACTS
YES	The town builds other sports areas for kids, like baseball diamonds.
YES	It'll keep skaters out of the empty pools in town.
YES	_____
YES	_____
YES	_____
NO	Pietown needs a toddler playground first.
NO	It might not be safe for new skaters.
NO	_____
NO	_____
NO	_____

So? What do YOU think?

Should Pietown open a skatepark?

Circle one: YES   NO

Fact & Opinion

Q: Should Sabeena stay best friends with Thalia?

First, READ Sabeena's diary.

Sabeena's Problem

Dear Diary:

I don't think I can be best friends with Thalia anymore. I mean, I know we've been friends since kindergarten, but people change. Like, we both used to love all the same things: Barbies, roller-skating, and playing pretend. But now, I'm really into soccer and ballet, while all Thalia can talk about is boys and computers.

On the other hand, it would be hard for us to stop being friends because we're next-door neighbors. I can just yell out the window when I want to hang out. Thalia always comes when you need her!

But she's a terrible friend! She borrows stuff and never gives it back—like my favorite hoodie. And she's definitely been telling lies about me behind my back at school.

When she's being nice, Thalia is so much fun. Nobody else knows how to cheer me up like she does. And our families are best friends too!

But still! The other day, when I beat her at volleyball, she pulled my hair. Who wants to be friends with a hair-puller?

Thanks for listening, Diary.

—Sabeena

Now, FILL IN the facts.

OPINION   **FACTS**

YES   They've been friends since kindergarten.

YES   _____

YES   _____

YES   _____

YES   _____

NO   They don't have the same interests anymore.

NO   _____

NO   _____

NO   _____

NO   _____

So? What do YOU think?

Should Sabeena stay best friends with Thalia?

Circle one: YES   NO

Q: Should animals be kept in zoos?

First, READ the news story.

Concrete Jungle

People have been arguing about zoos ever since the first zoo opened to the public in 1793. It's a real knock-down, drag-out fight!

"Zoos are not comfortable for animals. In a zoo, birds have their wings clipped so they can't fly," says animal rights activist Mr. Leon Fribble. "And elephants, that often walk 20 to 30 miles a day, only have a little bit of space to move around."

Zookeepers don't agree. "Animals in zoos are fed every day, and they're safe from attack," says Mr. Hyram Higgins of the Pietown Zoo. "We even have doctors to take care of them when they're sick."

Plus, Higgins adds, "Not only do scientists learn a lot from animals in zoos, but ordinary people come every day to watch animals they would never normally see. It's a great lesson!"

But Fribble and other activists don't think that the chance for learning is worth keeping animals captive. "What are we learning?" Fribble asks. "These animals aren't living naturally. In the wild, their behavior is all about finding food. In zoos, they don't need to hunt, they don't need to make their own homes. They're not doing anything! Except maybe going a little crazy."

Fribble points out that animals living in small spaces, with humans constantly staring at them, can develop strange behaviors. For instance, animals might walk in the same circle all day long, or try to hurt themselves.

"Animals don't act like that in the wild. The only way you can learn about them is by watching them in their natural habitats," says Fribble.

But how many families can visit Africa to see a lion in the wild?

"We no longer live with many wild animals, like in the old days," says Higgins. "We've killed off most of the wolves and the bears and the buffalo. Zoos are our only chance to be near them."

The greatest benefit that zoos can give to animals is species preservation. Since the 1970s, zoos have worked hard to breed animals that are endangered. But their success has been limited. Only a few wild animals can survive being born and raised in captivity.

Some people think it would be better to preserve the animals' natural habitats.

"After all," says environmentalist Ms. Sindy Hoo, "if we save a jungle or a swamp, it's not just good for the animals that live there. It's good for the whole planet!"

Now, turn the page to FILL IN the facts.

Now, FILL IN the facts.

OPINION	FACTS
YES	_____
YES	_____
YES	_____
YES	_____
YES	_____
NO	_____
NO	_____
NO	_____
NO	_____
NO	_____

So? What do YOU think?

Should animals be kept in zoos?

Circle one: YES   NO

✓ Check It!

Cut out the Check It! to see if you got the answers right.

Read between the Lines

CHOOSE a story to read, and try to catch when the author is being tricky—
telling you stuff without saying it straight out. WRITE DOWN the clues.

Title of story _____

What is the author talking about? _____

_____

_____

_____

What words does the author NOT use? _____

_____

_____

_____

So how did you figure it out? _____

_____

_____

_____

Read between the Lines

CHOOSE a story to read, and try to catch when the author is being tricky—telling you stuff without saying it straight out. WRITE DOWN the clues.

Title of story _____

What is the author talking about? _____

_____

_____

_____

_____

What words does the author NOT use? _____

_____

_____

_____

_____

So how did you figure it out? _____

_____

_____

_____

_____

Fact & Opinion

PICK a new nonfiction story or book to read today. As you read, FILL OUT this worksheet.

Topic:_____

OPINIONS	FACTS
_____	_____
_____	_____
_____	_____
_____	_____
_____	_____
_____	_____
_____	_____
_____	_____
_____	_____
_____	_____
_____	_____
_____	_____
_____	_____
_____	_____
_____	_____
_____	_____

Fact & Opinion

PICK a new nonfiction story or book to read today. As you read, FILL OUT this worksheet.

Topic:_____

OPINIONS	FACTS
_____	_____
_____	_____
_____	_____
_____	_____
_____	_____
_____	_____
_____	_____
_____	_____
_____	_____
_____	_____
_____	_____
_____	_____
_____	_____
_____	_____

Skimming

They say a picture's worth a thousand words. Especially if it's a graph, a chart, or a map. When you're skimming an article, don't forget to slap your eyes on the pictures. SKIM this article.

HINT: Notice anything funny about this page? We've already blurred the words you can skip.

Pizza Time in Pietown

Pizza's Popular Seven Days a Week

Riusting ero euis auguer sed min laoper dlit, consequ amconum e dio consectem doloreet num deli te digna feum ex eu faccum in at Riusting ero euis augeur sed min laoper dlit, consequ amconum e dio consectem doloreet num deli te digna feum ex eu faccum in at

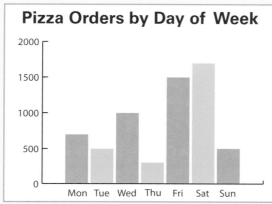

Pizza Orders by Day of Week

Friday and Saturday Rush!

Riusting ero euis auguer sed min ullaor secte velusting ero euis auguer sed mi laoper dlit, consequ amconum ex euguer. illaroper dlit, consequ amconum dio consectem doloreet num deliquat aut lummdo consectem doloreet num de

Thursday Is NOT Pizza Night

Riusting ero euis auguer sed min ullaor secte velusting ero euis auguer sed min laoper dlit, consequ amconum ex euguer. illaroper dlit, consequ amconum dio consectem doloreet num deliquat aut lummdo consectem doloreet num del

Now, CIRCLE the right answers to these questions.

1. Which is the most popular night for pizza in Pietown?
   a. Monday   b. Saturday   c. Friday

2. Which two days had the same number of pizza deliveries?
   a. Friday and Saturday   b. Monday and Thursday
   c. Tuesday and Sunday

3. Which day has the least number of pizza deliveries?
   a. Thursday   b. Sunday   c. Friday

You can learn a lot from a graph like this. Let's try some more!

✓ Check It!

Page 41

1. b
2. c
3. a

Page 43

1. b
2. a
3. c
4. a
5. b

Page 45

1. b
2. c
3. c
4. b
5. c

Pages 47-48

1. a
2. a
3. c
4. a
5. b
6. c
7. a
8. b
9. b
10. a

Skimming

SKIM this article.

What Is Pietown's Favorite Food?

Pietown Loves Pizza!

~~Riusting ero euis auguer sed min laorper cilit, consequ amconum dio consectem doloreet num de te digna feum ex eu faccum in e Riusting ero euis auguer sed min laorper cilit, consequ amconum Riusting ero euis auguer sed min laorper cilit, consequ amconum dio consectem doloreet num de te digna feum ex eu faccum in e~~

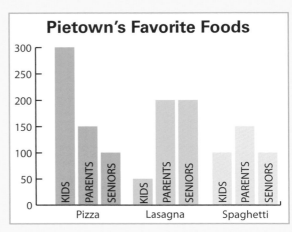

Pietown's Favorite Foods

French Fries Come in 4th with Kids!

~~Riusting ero euis auguer sed min ullaor secte veliusting ero euis auguer sed min laorper cilit, consequ amconum ex auguer. illalaorper cilit, consequ amconum dio consectem doloreet num deliquat aut lumndio consectem doloreet num de te digna feum ex eu faccum in et augiam.~~

Brussels Sprouts Lose Big

~~Riusting ero euis auguer sed min ullaor secte veliusting ero euis auguer sed min laorper cilit, consequ amconum ex auguer. illalaorper cilit, consequ amconum dio consectem doloreet num deliquat aut lumndio consectem doloreet num de te digna feum ex eu faccum in et augiam.~~

READ each question, and CHECK the right answer.

1. What kind of food do parents like most?

   a. Pizza

   b. Lasagna

   c. Spaghetti

2. What about kids? What's their favorite?

   a. Pizza

   b. Lasagna

   c. Spaghetti

3. What dish came in fourth place?

   a. Chicken fingers

   b. Cherry pie

   c. French fries

4. What kind of food won the most votes overall?

   a. Pizza

   b. Lasagna

   c. Spaghetti

5. Did many people vote for Brussels sprouts?

   a. Yes

   b. No

Skimming

SKIM this article.

Pietown Pizza Tasting Contest

Five Celebrity Judges Taste Toppings

Flusting ero euis auguer sed min ullao sacte velusting ero euis augluer sed min ullao laorger cilit, consequ amconum ex euguerc illaraorger cilit, consequ amconum ex eu dio consectem doloreet num deliquat aut lummdo consectem dolorest num deliquat te digna feum ex eu faccum in et augiam.

Pie Name	Topping Combo	Rating (out of 5)
Bad Breath Special	● ◆ ▲	★★★★⌐
Valentino	● ✦	★★★
Fruity Delite	▪ ✚	★★⌐
All U Need	◆ ▪ ▼ ✦	★★★★★
Something Fishy	▼ ▲ ◆	★★★★⌐
The Works	▪ ● ◆ ▼ ✚ ▲ ✦	★⌐

Olives Dropped This Year

Flusting ero euis augluer sed min ullao sacte velusting ero euis augluer sed min ullao laorger cilit, consequ amconum ex euguerc illaraorger cilit, consequ amconum ex eu dio consectem doloreet num deliquat aut lummdo consectem dolorest num deliquat te digna feum ex eu faccum in et augiam.

Who Puts CHERRIES on Pizza?

Flusting ero euis augluer sed min ullao sacte velusting ero euis augluer sed min ullao laorger cilit, consequ amconum ex euguerc illaraorger cilit, consequ amconum ex eu dio consectem doloreet num deliquat aut lummdo consectem dolorest num deliquat te digna feum ex eu faccum in et augiam.

Toppings Legend:

▪ = pineapple   ✚ = cherries

● = pepperoni   ▲ = sardines

◆ = garlic   ✦ = extra cheese

▼ = shrimp

READ each question, and CHECK the right answer.

1. How many of the pizzas DON'T have garlic?

   a. One

   b. Two

   c. Three

2. Which topping was dropped this year?

   a. Sausage

   b. Broccoli

   c. Olives

3. What was the highest rated pizza?

   a. Bad Breath Special

   b. The Works

   c. All U Need

4. What was the lowest rated pizza?

   a. Fruity Delite

   b. The Works

   c. Valentino

5. How many judges voted?

   a. Three

   b. Four

   c. Five

Skimming

SKIM this article.

Welcome to Pietown!

In Pietown, Pizza Rules

Riusting ero euis auguer sed min ullaor secte welusting ero euis auguer sed min ullaor laoger dilit, consequ amconum ex euguer: illaraoger dilit, consequ amconum ex euq dio consectem doloreet num deliquat aut lumndio consectem doloreet num deliquat te digna feum ex eu faccum in et augiam.

Pietown High: The Oldest Building in the State

Riusting ero euis auguer sed min ullaor secte welusting ero euis auguer sed min ullaor laoger dilit, consequ amconum ex euguer: illaraoger dilit, consequ amconum ex euq dio consectem doloreet num deliquat aut lumndio consectem doloreet num deliquat te digna feum ex eu faccum in et augiam.

Pietown's Famous Purple Houses

Riusting ero euis auguer sed min iusting ero euis auguer sed min ullaor secte went laoger dilit, consequ amconum exoger dilit, consequ amconum ex euguer: illamet dio consectem doloreet num deliqo consectem doloreet num deliquat aut lummod ing ero euis auguer sed min u er dilit, consequ amconum ex onsectem doloreet num deliqu ;ero euis auguer sed min ullao dilit, consequ amconum ex euq ectem doloreet num deliquat: ffeum ex eu faccum in et augia auguer sed min ullaor secte w equ amconum ex euguer: illa doreet num deliquat aut lumm eu faccum in et augiam.

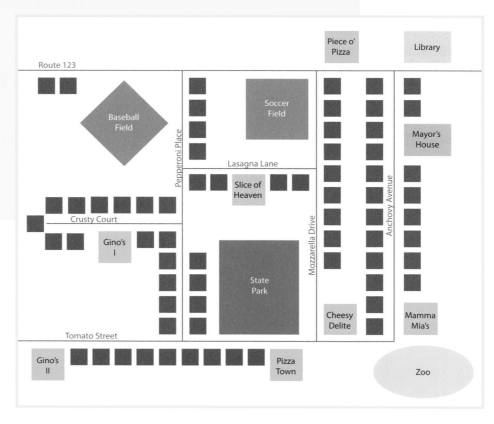

READ each question, and CHECK the right answer.

1. Which street do you take to get from Gino's II to Pizzatown?

   a. Tomato Street

   b. Route 123

   c. Anchovy Avenue

2. Which street is the longest?

   a. Route 123

   b. Pepperoni Place

   c. Lasagna Lane

3. What makes Pietown's houses so famous?

   a. They're really big.

   b. They're shaped like pizzas.

   c. They're purple.

4. What street should you live on if you don't want to be near any sports?

   a. Anchovy Avenue

   b. Crusty Court

   c. Mozarella Drive

5. What's the closest pizza place to the Pietown High?

   a. Pizza Town

   b. Gino's I

   c. Slice of Heaven

READ each question, and CHECK the right answer.

6. Which street does not have a pizza place?

   a. Route 123

   b. Lasagna Lane

   c. Pepperoni Place

7. How many pizza places do you pass when you go from the library to the high school?

   a. One

   b. Two

   c. Four

8. Which is the oldest building in the state?

   a. The Mayor's House

   b. Pietown High

   c. Mama Mia Pizzeria

9. To which pizza place do you think the zookeeper goes most often?

   a. Cheesy Delite

   b. Mama Mia's

   c. Piece o' Pizza

10. Which street has the most purple houses?

    a. Anchovy Avenue

    b. Tomato Street

    c. Pepperoni Place

Sometimes an article gives you a lot of information. To keep track of it all, look for the main ideas and the details. Then write them down. Here's how.

READ this article.

Topic: Fan Worship

When it comes to sports and music, people go a little crazy. For instance, fans of Wisconsin's Green Bay Packers football team have sold out every home game since 1960. They're known as "cheeseheads" because they wear foam cheese hats on their heads. Some of the male fans even go shirtless to games in the middle of winter!

Rock music has big fans too. The early 1960s were famous for "Beatlemania," where crowds of fans screamed so loud at Beatles concerts that no one could hear the music. Later fans of the Grateful Dead (called "Dead Heads") followed their favorite band all over the country. Two famous Dead Heads are ice cream makers Ben & Jerry, who named the flavor "Cherry Garcia" after Jerry Garcia, the lead singer of the Grateful Dead.

FILL IN the main ideas and details.

Main Idea 1

_____

Details

1. _____

2. _____

Main Idea 2

_____

Details

1. _____

2. _____

 **Check It!**

Page 49

Main idea 1: Sports

Details
1. Cheesehead Packer fans
2. Shirtless male fans in winter

Main idea 2: Music

Details
1. Beatlemania screaming fans
2. Dead Heads

Page 51

Main Idea 1:
Robbing the wrong place

Details:
1. bank that's closed or out of business
2. a police station

Main Idea 2:
Leaving your name and address

Details:
1. leaving a wallet
2. a medicine bottle
3. showing ID

Main Idea 3:
Botched getaways

Details:
1. falling asleep
2. broken getaway car
3. taking the bus
4. getting stuck in a duct

Check It!

Page 53

Main Idea 1: Bigfoot

Details:
1. has many names
2. really tall
3. covered in dark hair
4. face like gorilla
5. mascot of the 2010 Olympics
6. no proof

Main Idea 2: Loch Ness Monster

Details:
1. like a dragon or dinosaur
2. protected by the Scottish government
3. no proof

Main Idea 3: Jackalope

Details:
1. jackrabbit with antlers
2. milk can cure sickness
3. imitates human voice
4. might be caused by virus in real rabbits

Page 56

Main Idea 1: Kinds of magic

Details
1. sleight of hand
2. endurance
3. escapology (escape artists)
4. stage illusion
5. mentalism

Main Idea 2: Famous magic acts

Details
1. David Blaine
2. Penn & Teller
3. Harry Houdini
4. David Copperfield
5. Siegfried & Roy
6. The Amazing Kreskin

Main Idea 3: Tricks of the trade

Details
1. secret pockets
2. palming
3. rigged ropes
4. lock picks
5. mirrors
6. body doubles
7. shadows
8. manipulation
9. body language
10. collusion

READ the article.

Topic: Dumb Criminals

As if it wasn't dumb enough to turn to a life of crime! There are great stories about thieves who messed up big time. Here's some advice, based on true events.

Dumb criminals rob the wrong place at the wrong time. If you're a bank robber, you should probably rob a bank when it's open. You should also make sure that the bank you want to rob is still in business. It's also not a good idea to break into a police station.

One way to make sure you get caught is to leave behind your wallet or a bottle of prescription medication that has your name and address on it. One clever criminal even showed his driver's license to a store clerk before he stole a bottle of whiskey. (He had to prove he was over 21, after all!)

Don't forget the getaway! It's really dumb to fall asleep in the house you're robbing (even if the bed is comfortable). Make sure your getaway car is working (and filled with gas). Don't take the city bus. And here's an extra-special tip: If your plan involves crawling through a tight duct or pipe—go on a diet! Police get tired of rescuing would-be thieves who get stuck on their way in or out of a robbery.

Clearly, crime is stupid. And criminals are just plain DUMB.

FILL IN the main ideas and details.

Main Idea 1

_____

Details

1. _____

2. _____

Main Idea 2

_____

Details

1. _____

2. _____

3. _____

4. _____

Main Idea 3

_____

Details

1. _____

2. _____

3. _____

4. _____

READ the article.

Topic: Cryptids

Believe it or not, there's a word for the study of legendary creatures: *cryptozoology*. Monsters like Bigfoot and the Loch Ness Monster fall into this category. They are *cryptids*. But is there any proof that they exist?

Our hairy friend Bigfoot is known as *Sasquatch* in North America, *Yeren* in China, and *Yowie* in Australia. He really gets around! You'd recognize him right away. He's really tall (about 7 to 10 feet) and covered in dark hair, with a face like a gorilla. There's no concrete proof that he's real, but "Quatchi" is an official mascot of the 2010 Olympic Games in Vancouver.

Down in the dark depths of a lake in Scotland you'll find "Nessie," the Loch Ness Monster. She's been described as a creature like a dragon or a dinosaur. In spite of some photographs, movies, and sonar tests, no one can really prove she exists. But if she does, she'll be safe. Nessie's officially recognized by the Scottish government, and no one is allowed to hurt her.

Then there's the Jackalope—a jackrabbit with big antlers like an antelope. Legend says milk from a jackalope can cure sickness and that Jackalopes can imitate the human voice. However, experts believe that jackalopes really *do* exist, sort of. Rabbits can get a virus that gives them big, hornlike growths on their heads. From far away, these sick rabbits look just like Jackalopes!

FILL IN the main ideas and details.

Main Idea 1

_____

Details

1. _____

2. _____

3. _____

4. _____

5. _____

6. _____

Main Idea 2

_____

Details

1. _____

2. _____

3. _____

Main Idea 3

_____

Details

1. _____

2. _____

3. _____

4. _____

READ the article, then FILL IN the main idea and details on page 56.

Topic: The World of Illusion

The modern magic show has nothing to do with real magic. Everyone in the audience understands that the person on stage is only *pretending* to have magical powers. It's fun to watch and try to figure out how it's done! There are many kinds of magic, and lots of famous magicians who use different tricks of the trade.

The most common kind of magic is something you can learn to do yourself: *sleight of hand*. It takes a lot of practice, but when you're good at it, you can make things like cards or coins appear or disappear! It's all about pulling things out of secret pockets, or holding things in your hands (called *palming*) so that nobody sees what you're doing. Magicians like David Blaine and Penn & Teller became famous for their amazing skills at sleight of hand.

David Blaine is also famous as an *endurance artist*. He's been buried alive, sealed in ice, and held under water. And he survived! Most of the time, though, magicians called *escape artists* try to get out of these kind of situations. Some use rigged ropes or lock picks to do it. But other *escapologists* are simply very strong and flexible—they wriggle their way out. Harry Houdini was the most famous escape artist of all.

Another kind of magic is the kind of flashy *stage illusion* that you'll find at big theaters or on TV. In these shows, magicians make it seem like people are cut in half, float in midair, or disappear. Star illusionist David Copperfield has walked through the Great Wall of China and made the Statue of Liberty disappear! In Las Vegas, you once could watch Siegfried and Roy make their famous tigers appear out of nowhere. Most of the time, this kind of magic is done with mirrors, body doubles, shadows, or other special effects.

Mental magic is done by *mentalists* like the Amazing Kreskin. Mentalists try to read people's minds or hypnotize them on stage. Sometimes the mentalist manipulates an audience member or reads their body language to find an answer. Other times, the audience member is really a partner of the mentalist, and they've worked out their act beforehand. This is called *collusion*.

Stage magic is a combination of tricks, talent, and showmanship. The real magic comes when you can amaze the crowd and make them ask: "How'd he *do* that?"

Turn the page to fill in the main idea and details.

FILL IN the main ideas and details.

Main Idea 1

_____

Details

1. escapology _____

2. _____

3. _____

4. _____

5. _____

Main Idea 2

_____

Details

1. David Blaine _____

2. _____

3. _____

4. _____

5. _____

6. _____

Main Idea 3

Tricks of the Trade _____

Details

1. palming _____

2. _____

3. _____

4. _____

5. _____

6. _____

7. _____

8. _____

9. _____

10. _____

Main Idea & Details

PICK a new nonfiction article or book to read today. As you read, LOOK FOR the main ideas and details, and WRITE them on this sheet.

Main ideas	Details

Main Idea & Details

PICK a new nonfiction article or book to read today. As you read, LOOK FOR the main ideas and details, and WRITE them on this sheet.

Main ideas	Details

You know you've really read something when you can answer questions about it. Let's look at two kinds of questions: **Right There** and **Think & Search**.

READ this article.

> ### Long Live the Queen!
>
> Elizabeth II was only 25 when she became Queen of England after the death of her father, King George VI. She was crowned in 1952. Next in line for the throne is the Queen's son, Prince Charles. But since the Queen's mother (also a Queen Elizabeth) lived to be 101, Elizabeth II may reign for many more years!

The answer to a **Right There** question can be found in one sentence (or word).

1. How old was Elizabeth II when she became Queen?

   _____

See? The answer is "Right There!"

You'll find the answer to a **Think & Search** question in more than one place.

2. Who were Queen Elizabeth's parents?

   _____

   _____

You had to look around for that one, right?

Keep going. You'll never be afraid of a pop quiz again!

✓ Check It!

Page 59

1. 25
2. King George VI and Queen Elizabeth

Page 60

1. A: a drum kit
2. B: Charla, Quentin, Neil, Wanda, and Iris.
3. A: The AstroBunnies
4. B: drums, guitar, keyboards, bass violin, trumpet

Page 61

1. A: Yes.
2. A: Rodeo cowboys
3. B: Buster Keaton, Harold Lloyd, Helen Holmes, and Jackie Chan
4. B: pratfalls, horse riding, jumping onto a moving train, leaping off a building

Page 62

1. B: pilot, mayor, pizza chef
2. A: 18
3. Suggested Q: What toppings did Grandma try on her pizzas?
4. Suggested A: cherries, raisins, pudding, mustard, chocolate jimmies

Check It!

Page 63

1. A: Hula Hoop
2. B: swallowing goldfish, flagpole sitting, streaking, Cabbage Patch dolls
3. Suggested Q: How many people watched a man sit on a flagpole in 1929?
4. Suggested A: 20,000

Page 64

Suggestions.

1. Q: How old was Iggy when his strength was discovered?
   A: Three years old

2. Q: What can Iggy do because he's so strong?
   A: He throws a ball into the next town, crushes the checkers, cracks the house, and throws babysitters onto the roof.

Page 66

Suggestions.

1. A: Q: Who did Damen invite to his birthday party?
   A: All the kids in his class.
2. B: Q: What did the kids eat at Damen's party?
   A: barbecued burgers, hot dogs, chicken, soda, chips, cake, ice cream, and cupcakes.
3. A Q: How old was Damen?
   A: Ten years old.
4. B Q: What was there to do at Damen's party?
   A: swim in the pool, play volleyball and basketball, race go-carts, play arcade games and video games, eat
5. A Q: What happened after it got dark?
   A: There were fireworks and a cake with sparklers.

READ the story, then ANSWER the questions.

The Famous AstroBunnies

Have you ever heard of the AstroBunnies? It's a band that came to life the day I got a drum kit for my 12th birthday. My brother Quentin already had a guitar, and his best friend Neil played the keyboards. We practiced every afternoon in Neil's garage. One day, his next-door neighbor, Wanda, brought over her big standup bass violin. It sounded great! Then we were joined by Wanda's best friend Iris, who played the trumpet. We offered to play for free at my cousin Alfred's birthday party. But after our first song, my cousin yelled, "Hey Charla! How much do I have to pay you guys *not* to play at my party?" So we got $50 for our first gig! Pretty cool, huh?

A = Right There Question   *B = Think & Search Question*

MARK each question with an A or a B in the box. Then ANSWER the questions.

1. ☐ What did Charla get for her 12th birthday?

_____

2. ☐ Which kids were in the band?

_____

3. ☐ What's the name of the band?

_____

4. ☐ What instruments are in the band?

_____

READ the story, then ANSWER the questions.

Fall Guys and Fall Gals

Without stuntmen and women, action movies would be pretty boring. In the early days of film, actors like Buster Keaton and Harold Lloyd did their own silly pratfalls for their famous comedies. Makers of old western movies used rodeo cowboys as stuntmen because they knew how to ride (and fall off) horses. And it wasn't just men. In the silent movie series *The Hazards of Helen*, Helen Holmes jumped onto a moving train and leaped off a building! Nowadays trained professionals do the stunts for most actors, except when it's a Jackie Chan movie! This martial arts wizard always fights his own battles. He's got the broken bones to prove it!

A = Right There Question   B = Think & Search Question

MARK each question with an A or a B in the box. Then ANSWER the questions.

1. ☐ Do women do stunts?

_____

2. ☐ Who were some of the first stuntmen for westerns?

_____

3. ☐ Who are some actors that did their own stunts?

_____

4. ☐ What kinds of stunts were done in early movies?

_____

READ the story, then ANSWER the questions.

Mama Mia!

My Grandma Mia is an amazing woman. When she was 18, she got her pilot's license and flew all around the state, delivering packages and dropping plant food on crops for farmers. Later she went into politics and became the first female mayor of Pietown. After that, she started her favorite career: running Mama Mia's Pizzeria. She was the first pizza chef to try putting cherries on pizza. It was a hit! She's also tried toppings like raisins, pudding, and mustard. But her favorite pizza topping is chocolate jimmies. Yum!

A = Right There Question   B = Think & Search Question

MARK each question with an A or a B in the box. Then ANSWER the questions.

1. ☐   What jobs has Grandma had in her life?

   _____

2. ☐   How old was Grandma when she got her pilot's license?

   _____

Now, FILL IN this blank with one more **Think & Search** question:

3. _____

What's the answer?

4. _____

READ the story, then ANSWER the questions.

Just a Fad

The twentieth century was known for a lot of crazy fads. A fad is something that everybody wants to do or watch—for a short while. It's also called a *craze*, and they can be pretty crazy! Take swallowing goldfish, for example. In the 1940s, college students competed to see how many little flippers they could scarf down. Think that's weird? In 1929, 20,000 people watched a man sit on a flagpole for 49 days! The Hula Hoop was the famous fad toy of the 1950s. Cabbage Patch dolls ruled the 1980s. Toy fads are way better than stripping naked and running around, which was the fad of the 1970s (called *streaking*). Can you think of any fads that happened during *your* lifetime?

A = Right There Question   B = Think & Search Question

MARK each question with an A or a B in the box. Then ANSWER the questions.

1. [ ] What was the toy fad of the 1950s?

_____

2. [ ] What crazy activities became fads in the twentieth century?

_____

Now, FILL IN this blank with one more **Right There** question:

3. _____

What's the answer?

4. _____

READ the story, then ANSWER the questions.

The Strongest Kid in the World

When my little brother Ignacio was three years old, he picked up the family SUV and held it in the air for a full minute. That's when we knew he was the strongest kid in the world. It's tricky living with him. Iggy likes to play ball, but sometimes he throws the ball into the next town! If you try to play checkers with him, he accidentally crushes the pieces in his hands. And when he gets mad—watch out! One time, Iggy kicked the floor so hard, it cracked our house down the middle. Any time he gets mad at a babysitter he tosses her onto the roof, and we have to call the fire department to get her down. More than any other kid, Iggy needs to learn how to play nice!

1. What's a **Right There** question you could ask about Iggy?

_____

What's the answer?

_____

2. What's a **Think & Search** question you could ask about Iggy?

_____

What's the answer?

_____

READ the story, then ANSWER the questions on the next page.

Pool Party

For his tenth birthday, Damen Escondido had a giant pool party at his parents' mansion on the rich side of town. He invited all the kids in his grade at school. There was so much to do! He had three inter-connected swimming pools with slides, tunnels, and waterfalls. The house was surrounded by acres of green grass with volleyball and basketball courts. There was even a track for go-cart races!

Inside the house, there was a room full of arcade games (that you didn't have to pay for!) and a huge TV with all the video games you've ever heard of. We ignored the yucky grownup food and ate barbecued burgers, hot dogs, and chicken with tons of soda and chips. When it got dark, Damen's parents had a fireworks show and brought out a cake that must have been five feet tall! It was covered with sparklers. There was ice cream to go with the cake and cupcakes for all of us to take home. I don't think I've ever had so much in my entire life! Too bad I never got a chance to meet Damen. I bet he's a nice kid.

Turn the page to answer the questions.

FILL IN the blanks with questions of each type. Then ANSWER the questions.

A = Right There Question   B = Think & Search Question

1. **A** _____

_____

2. **B** _____

_____

3. **A** _____

_____

4. **B** _____

_____

5. **A** _____

_____

You've got **Right There** and **Think and Search** questions all figured out. Now it's time to tackle two more kinds of questions: **On Your Own** and **Author and Me**.

READ this story.

Worst Birthday Ever?

What a rotten birthday! All of Eli's friends had something else to do today—something secret. Even his parents had gone out! There were no plans for a special dinner or a cake. Worst of all, Eli's mom told him to take his little sister to the bowling alley for the afternoon. The whole way there, she kept giggling and saying: "I know something you don't know."

Eli sighed as he opened the door to the bowling alley.

Only YOU can answer an **On Your Own** question.

1. How would you feel if your birthday started out like this?

Anytime a question asks for your thoughts or imagination, you need to answer the question **On Your Own**.

You need to read between the lines to answer an **Author and Me** question.

2. What do you think will happen at the bowling alley?

The author gave you clues, and you figured out the rest!

Ready to try some more? Let's go!

Check It!

Page 67

Suggestions:
1. sad, angry, lonely
2. Eli's friends and family are throwing him a surprise party.

Page 68

1. C
2. D: Against.
3. C: Write your own opinion.
4. D: A rabbit doesn't have to be smuggled into the country, and it won't get big and dangerous.

Page 69

1. D: Snow White.
2. C: Yes or no.
3. C: What did you name your dwarves?
4. D: No way! He's got bad breath and a bald spot. Plus, she hardly knows him!

Page 70

1. C: Chocolate bars or cocoa —which did you pick?
2. D: Because they invented the chocolate bar and eat the most chocolate.
3. Suggested Q: Do you like chocolate?
4. Suggested A: Yes!

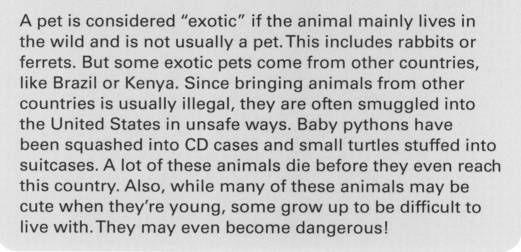

READ the story, then
ANSWER the questions.

Exotic Pets

A pet is considered "exotic" if the animal mainly lives in the wild and is not usually a pet. This includes rabbits or ferrets. But some exotic pets come from other countries, like Brazil or Kenya. Since bringing animals from other countries is usually illegal, they are often smuggled into the United States in unsafe ways. Baby pythons have been squashed into CD cases and small turtles stuffed into suitcases. A lot of these animals die before they even reach this country. Also, while many of these animals may be cute when they're young, some grow up to be difficult to live with. They may even become dangerous!

C = On Your Own Question   D = Author and Me Question

MARK each question with a C or a D in the box. Then ANSWER the questions.

1. [C] Would you like to have an exotic pet?

_____

2. [D] Is this article for or against smuggling exotic pets from other countries?

_____

3. [ ] What kind of exotic pet would you like to have?

_____

4. [ ] Why is owning a tiger worse than having a rabbit?

_____

READ the story, then ANSWER the questions.

First Kiss

I opened my eyes to see a young man in a fancy hat breathing down on me.

"It worked!" he cried.

The dwarves began to dance with glee. "She's awake!" they hollered.

The man held out his hand and bowed. He had a bald spot on his head. "Princess," he said, "my kiss has saved you from that evil poisoned apple."

Too bad your breath nearly killed me, I thought.

Then he got down on his knees. The dwarves fell silent. "Will you be my wife, Princess?"

Why couldn't he have let me sleep?

C = On Your Own Question   D = Author and Me Question

MARK each question with a C or a D in the box. THEN answer the questions.

1. [ ] Who is this princess?

_____

2. [ ] Would you like to be a prince or princess?

_____

3. [ ] If you had seven dwarves, what would you name them?

_____

4. [ ] Do you think the princess will marry the man? Why or why not?

_____

READ the story, then ANSWER the questions.

A Delicious History

Chocolate has been around for 2000 years. The ancient Mayans called it *xocolatl*, which means "bitter water." For most of its history, chocolate was a drink, not a solid. It's made from the seeds of the cacao tree, found in South America. Christopher Columbus brought some cocao seeds back with him when he returned from the New World. People in Europe fell in love with it! Chocolate drinks were expensive and mainly for the rich. Definitely for adults only! The Pilgrims thought chocolate was sinful and banned it from the Plymouth colony. Finally, a Swiss chocolate maker created a solid chocolate bar around 1875. Today the average American eats 10 to 12 pounds of chocolate a year. But in Switzerland, everybody eats about 21 pounds a year. After all, they're the chocolate experts!

C = On Your Own Question   D = Author and Me Question

MARK each question with a C or a D in the box. Then ANSWER the questions.

1. ☐ Which do you like better, chocolate bars or hot cocoa?

   _____

2. ☐ Why are Swiss people such chocolate experts?

   _____

Now, FILL IN this blank with one more **On Your Own** question:

3. _____

What's the answer?

4. _____

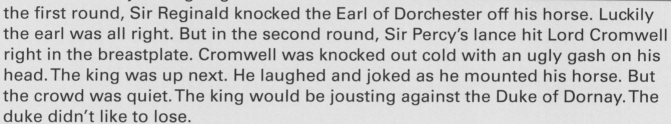

READ the story, then ANSWER the questions.

A Dangerous Game

Everyone except the king was nervous as the jousting began. In the first round, Sir Reginald knocked the Earl of Dorchester off his horse. Luckily the earl was all right. But in the second round, Sir Percy's lance hit Lord Cromwell right in the breastplate. Cromwell was knocked out cold with an ugly gash on his head. The king was up next. He laughed and joked as he mounted his horse. But the crowd was quiet. The king would be jousting against the Duke of Dornay. The duke didn't like to lose.

Sir Bryan Howard raced over to the duke as he got on his horse. "Listen man!" he hissed. "Remember, the king does not yet have an heir."

C = On Your Own Question   D = Author and Me Question

MARK each question with a C or a D in the box. Then ANSWER the questions.

1. [ ] Why is everyone so nervous about the joust?

   _____

2. [ ] What do you think of jousting?

   _____

Now, FILL IN this blank with one more **Author and Me** question:

3. _____

What's the answer?

4. _____

READ the story, then ANSWER the questions.

The Ghost of Cabin 8

Halfway through the summer, a ghost moved into Cabin 8. Keenan saw it first. He said it was short and wore a black mask. A few nights later, Oscar saw the ghost jumping off a table. It had fluffy fur and a long ringed tail. Casey didn't see it, but he heard the ghost making a high-pitched chattering sound like a monkey. The next day, all the food that they kept hidden in the cabin was torn open and eaten!

"It was the ghost!" said Keenan.

"Look!" cried Jeremy. "I bet it got in through that hole in the screen door."

"But ghosts don't use doors," Casey pointed out.

The boys didn't know what to think. Do you?

A = Right There Question   B = Think & Search Question

C = On Your Own Question   D = Author and Me Question

MARK each question with an A, B, C or D in the box. Then ANSWER the questions.

1. ☐ What was "haunting" Cabin 8?

   _____

2. ☐ Who saw the ghost first?

   _____

3. ☐ Are you afraid of ghosts?

   _____

4. ☐ What did the ghost look like?

   _____

READ this article, then ANSWER the questions.

Be Lean, Clean, and GREEN!

Everybody's talking about the weather these days. Is it getting hotter? Have humans hurt the planet? And here's the really important question: What can I do to help fix things?

Believe it or not, kids are the best army we have to fight this problem. Why? Because when they grow up, kids will be stuck with this planet, this weather, and all these other problems. There are a lot of things kids can do—starting right now.

First of all, LEARN. Pair up with a grownup to surf the web, read books or newspapers, and talk to experts. If you don't know what "carbon gas" or "climate change" means, those are good places to start.

Next, *act*. Start with simple things you can do, like using fluorescent light bulbs, planting a tree, recycling, and taking the bus or your bike to school. Find out how much water and electricity your family uses. Count how many trash bags go out every week. Come up with a plan to cut down on waste in your house.

Finally, *share*. Spread the word! Tell your friends, your family, your neighbors. Be the greenest kid on the block—and brag about it! Start a contest to see who can make the most change.

Because change is what it's all about!

Now, turn the page and answer the questions.

FILL IN the blanks with questions of each type. Then ANSWER the questions.

A = Right There Question   *B = Think & Search Question*

C = On Your Own Question   *D = Author and Me Question*

1. | A | _____

_____

2. | B | _____

_____

3. | C | _____

_____

4. | D | _____

_____

5. | C | _____

_____

Question Busters!

Next time you've finished reading a story or article, WRITE four questions about it. Then ANSWER your own questions. For each question, DECIDE what kind it is and WRITE an A, B, C, or D in the box.

A = Right There Question   *B = Think & Search Question*

C = On Your Own Question   *D = Author and Me Question*

The title of my reading is _____

Questions

1. ⬚ _____
2. ⬚ _____
3. ⬚ _____
4. ⬚ _____

Answers

1. _____

_____

2. _____

_____

3. _____

_____

4. _____

_____

Question Busters!

Next time you've finished reading a story or article, WRITE four questions about it. Then ANSWER your own questions. For each question, DECIDE what kind it is and WRITE an A, B, C, or D in the box.

A = Right There Question   *B = Think & Search Question*

C = On Your Own Question   *D = Author and Me Question*

The title of my reading is _____

Questions

1. _____
2. _____
3. _____
4. _____

Answers

1. _____
   _____
2. _____
   _____
3. _____
   _____
4. _____
   _____

Question Busters!

Next time you've finished reading a story or article, WRITE four questions about it. Then ANSWER your own questions. For each question, DECIDE what kind it is and WRITE an A, B, C, or D in the box.

A = Right There Question   *B = Think & Search Question*

C = On Your Own Question   *D = Author and Me Question*

The title of my reading is _____

Questions

1. ☐ _____
2. ☐ _____
3. ☐ _____
4. ☐ _____

Answers

1. _____

_____

2. _____

_____

3. _____

_____

4. _____

_____

Question Busters!

Next time you've finished reading a story or article, WRITE four questions about it. Then ANSWER your own questions. For each question, DECIDE what kind it is and WRITE an A, B, C, or D in the box.

A = Right There Question   *B = Think & Search Question*

C = On Your Own Question   *D = Author and Me Question*

The title of my reading is _____

Questions

1. [ ] _____
2. [ ] _____
3. [ ] _____
4. [ ] _____

Answers

1. _____

_____

2. _____

_____

3. _____

_____

4. _____

_____

Compare & Contrast

Another great way to keep track of your facts is to COMPARE and CONTRAST. This helps you find differences between two similar subjects or similarities between two different subjects. You might even be surprised by what you find out!

FILL IN the blanks with these hockey facts.

| J-shaped stick | L-shaped stick | Hit ball |
| Score goals | Players wear pads | Hit puck |

Ice Hockey   Both   Field Hockey

play on ice	use hockey sticks	play on grass
_____	_____	_____
_____	_____	_____

See? When you compare and contrast these two subjects, you figure out how to tell them apart, and what they have in common.

Compare & Contrast

✓ Check It!

Page 84

MovieBox: comfy seats, fresh popcorn, slushies, boring movies
Royale: bigger screens, stale popcorn, better movies
Both: six screens, serve popcorn, show too many previews

Page 85

Mountain Bike: good for riding through woods, wide tires, shocks, good for going uphill, can change gears
BMX Bike: good for doing tricks, smaller frame, spinning handlebars, no gears
Both: strong bikes, go off-road, expensive, fun

Page 86

Tiger Woods: #1 golf champion, still competing
Michael Jordan: best basketball player ever, 12 years older, retired
Both: world-class athletes, play golf, went pro at 21, have African-American dads, have Nike shoe line, started charitable foundations

Page 88

1. **Sharks:** fish, no bones, breath through gills, silent
2. **Dolphins:** always have teeth, clicks and whistles
3. **Whales:** some have teeth, some have baleen, some sing mating songs, prefer salt water
4. **All:** live in water, fusiform body, carnivores
5. **Sharks/Dolphins:** some live in fresh water
6. **Sharks/Whales:** some are filter feeders
7. **Dolphins/Whales:** cetacea, breathe through blowholes

READ the paragraph, then FILL IN the blanks.

HINT: The facts are highlighted.

Comet or Asteroid?

Our solar system includes comets and asteroids. What's the difference? Comets are made up of ice and dust. When they get close to the sun, the ice melts, and the comet forms a tail of junk behind it as it falls apart. Asteroids, however, are made up of rocks and metals that stay together. Both comets and asteroids have an *elliptical* (oval) orbit around the sun. But while asteroids go around in the same direction as all the planets, comets go whichever way they want. Asteroids like to hang out together in the asteroid belt between Mars and Jupiter. Unlike asteroids, you can see some comets with your own two eyes! And you can always enjoy the meteor showers that both comets and asteroids give us here on Earth when they fly by.

Comets   **Both**   **Asteroids**

_____   _____   _____

_____   _____   _____

_____   _____

_____

READ the paragraph, then FILL IN the blanks.

HINT: The facts are highlighted.

Storm Warning

There's a big storm rattling your windows—is it a tornado or a hurricane? Hurricanes form over the ocean, gaining power from the water, while tornados mostly form over land. Tornados are pretty skinny—they can only get as wide as 1.5 miles. But hurricanes are sometimes hundreds of miles across! A hurricane can also last for days. Tornados don't usually last for more than an hour, but they can be STRONG, with much faster winds than a hurricane. Both storms are bad news, causing floods and damage wherever they go. Hurricanes and tornados have one other thing in common: they both spin counterclockwise in the Northern Hemisphere and clockwise in the Southern Hemisphere!

Tornadoes   **Both**   **Hurricanes**

Compare & Contrast

READ the paragraph, then FILL IN the blanks.

Not-So-Identical Twins

Judy and Junie were born five minutes apart. They're identical twins, but I have no trouble telling them apart. It's true! Even though they have the same brown eyes and long black hair, I know right away who's who. See, Judy usually wears her hair in a ponytail, and Junie has her ears pierced. And they may have the same nose, but Judy has a red birthmark to the left of it, while Junie doesn't. Plus, Junie always wears green. Their voices are identical, but Judy's got a whacky hyena laugh. Junie's really quiet, always writing in her journal. And Judy's crazy about music. I don't think they're alike at all, really!

Judy   Both   Junie

READ the paragraph, then FILL IN the blanks.

Buckle Up!

Both of my parents are safe drivers, but they've got totally different styles. Dad drives fast (sometimes a little too fast) and stops suddenly. Mom drives slow (sometimes a little too slow), and she stops gradually. In the car, they both listen to the radio, but Dad blasts rock music, while Mom listens to talk radio. Mom also likes to have the car windows open. Sometimes she leans out and yells to people she knows on the street. Ugh! Dad pumps up the AC and drums his hands on the steering wheel. They both love to drive. But Mom makes me nervous sometimes because, when she talks to me, she stops looking at the road. I always have to remind her she's driving!

Mom's Driving   **Both**   **Dad's Driving**

Compare & Contrast

READ the paragraph, then FILL IN the blanks.

Movie Night

Pietown has two movie theaters: the Royale and the MovieBox. They have six screens each. My favorite is MovieBox, but my best friend Gil says Royale is best. I don't see why! The screens at Royale are bigger, but the seats at the MovieBox are way more comfortable. And the popcorn at the MovieBox is fresh. The Royale serves stale popcorn. AND Royale doesn't have Slushies! On the other hand, the Royale does get better movies, mostly action and horror. Sometimes, the MovieBox only has boring romances or movies from other countries. And they both show too many previews!

MovieBox   Both   Royale

_____   _____   _____

_____   _____   _____

_____   _____   _____

_____

READ the paragraph, then FILL IN the blanks.

Bike Shopping

When you're looking for your next pair of all-terrain wheels, you need to decide whether you want a mountain bike or a bicycle motocross. They're both really strong bikes that can take a lot of banging around. And they both go off-road (or off-sidewalk). The mountain bike has wider tires that work great in the woods. It also has shock absorbers to help you bounce through those bumps. But if tricks are your thing, get a BMX! Its smaller frame and spinning handlebars are great for showing off your stuff. But you can't change gears on a BMX so—if you'll be going uphill—you should get a mountain bike. They're both pretty expensive, though. And a lot of fun!

Mountain Bike   **Both**   **BMX Bike**

_____   _____   _____

_____   _____   _____

_____   _____   _____

_____   _____   _____

_____

Compare & Contrast

READ the paragraph, then FILL IN the blanks.

Two of a Kind

When Tiger Woods plays golf for fun, who would you guess is his favorite partner? Michael Jordan, that's who! Both of these world-class athletes play golf. But while Tiger is the world's number one golfer, Michael Jordan is considered the best basketball player of all time. They both went pro when they were 21, and they both had African-American dads. And, of course, there's a Nike shoe line for each of them. They also have foundations that raise money to help people in need: the Tiger Woods Foundation and the James Jordan Foundation (in honor of Mike's dad). These two golf buddies weren't separated at birth, though—Mike is 12 years older than Tiger, and he's retired. Tiger will still be swinging for a while!

Tiger **Both** **Michael**

_____ _____ _____

_____ _____ _____

_____ _____

_____

_____

READ the article, then FILL IN the blanks on the next page.

The Deep Blue Three

In the deep blue sea live the deep blue three: sharks, whales, and dolphins. They all live in the water, and they look alike because of their *fusiform* (streamlined) bodies. But there're lots of differences!

Dolphins and whales are both part of the *cetacean* family. But dolphins always have teeth. Some whales don't have teeth. Instead, these *baleen* whales have a comb-like filter (called a *baleen*) so they can swim around with their mouths open, collecting fish to eat. That's called *filter feeding*. Some sharks are filter feeders too!

Unlike dolphins and whales, sharks are fish. And get this: sharks don't have any bones! They've got cartilage instead, which is strong but bendable (like your nose). Sharks breathe water through their gills. Dolphins and whales have to breathe air through their blowholes.

Humpbacks and other whales are famous for their mating songs. Dolphins don't sing, but they use clicks and whistles to help them find each other and figure out where they are in the ocean. Sharks are silent—the better to sneak up on their prey!

The deep blue three are carnivores, which means they eat other living creatures. There are some dolphins and sharks that can live in fresh water, like rivers. But there aren't any baleen whales who can survive in fresh water for very long. They like it salty!

Turn the page and fill in the blanks.

Compare & Contrast

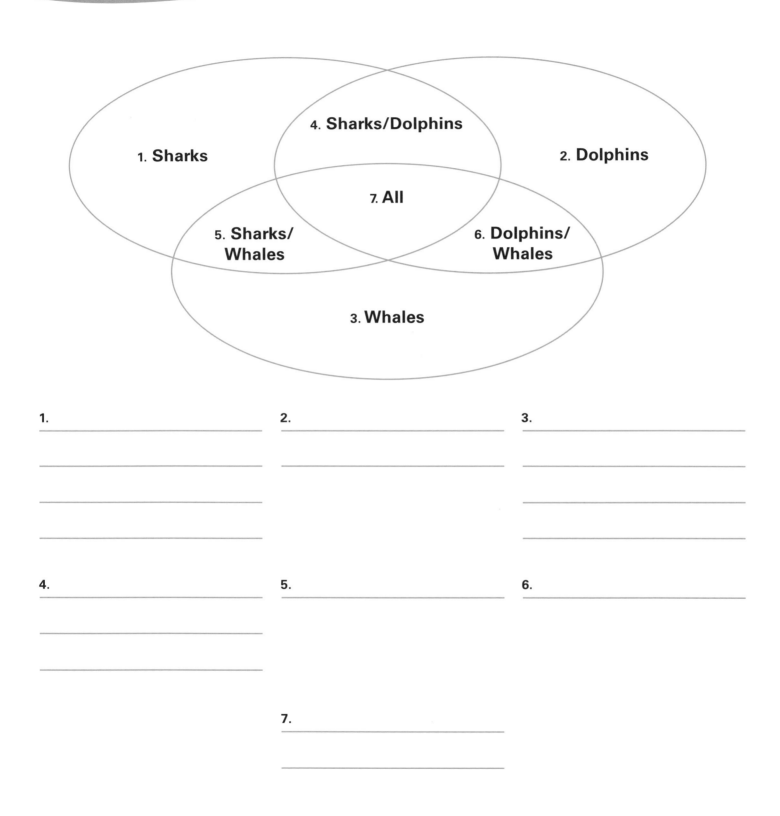

1. Sharks

4. Sharks/Dolphins

2. Dolphins

7. All

5. Sharks/ Whales

6. Dolphins/ Whales

3. Whales

1. _____

2. _____

3. _____

4. _____

5. _____

6. _____

7. _____

10

There's lots of information in fiction stories: setting, main characters, problems, solutions. To keep track of it all, make a STORY PLAN. After you've filled out a story plan, you'll have a quickie version of the story right there to help you remember everything that happened. Check it out!

FILL IN the missing information in this story plan. We've gotten you started.

Cinderella Goes to the Ball

The story takes place <u>once upon a time, in a land far, far away</u>.

1 _____ is a character in the story who <u>has a mean stepmother and two ugly stepsisters</u>. 2 _____

_____

is another character in this story who has a magic wand.

The first thing that happens in the story is that <u>Cinderella finds out there's going to be a ball at the prince's castle</u>.

A problem occurs when 3 _____

_____.

After that, <u>Cinderella's fairy godmother appears and offers to help but Cinderella has nothing to wear and no way to get to the ball</u>. The problem is solved when 4 _____

_____.

The story ends with 5 _____

_____.

Now that you're all warmed up, let's do some more!

Story Plan

Check It!

Page 97

Title: Down in the Basement
1. in an apartment building
2. Cassie
3. moves into a new apartment building
4. Cassie's mother
5. wants Cassie to be happy
6. Cassie hates her new apartment building
7. Cassie can't find any kids her own age in the building
8. Cassie discovers a room in the basement where all the kids play together
9. Cassie pretending to be a princess with another girl her age

Page 100

Title: Robinson Family Vacation
1. on the Pacific Ocean in the summer
2. Lionel Robinson
3. loves to play video games and hates sailing
4. The rest of the Robinson family
5. love sailing
6. The Robinsons plan to go on a sailing vacation for 2 months
7. a storm wrecks the Robinson's boat
8. the Robinsons wash up on a desert island
9. Their radio isn't working so they can't get help
10. Lionel uses the batteries from his video game to make the radio work again
11. the Robinsons being rescued and Lionel spending the rest of the summer playing video games

READ the story.

The Pirates of Pieville

In the 1700s, Pieville was filled with pirates. In fact, it used to be called "Pirateville." The town was a mess! The pirates were always fighting and stealing and digging for buried treasure.

Percy the Pirate was the worst. When he was at sea, he'd shoot down any ship he saw, then kidnap the people on board. One day, he captured a sailor from Italy named Sergio Minnatti. Sergio was funny, and he played the guitar, so Percy took him back to Pirateville to be his personal musician. Sergio loved playing for the pirates! One day, Percy was really hungry after a day of digging for treasure. But when he came home, he found that his cook had been kidnapped by another pirate gang.

"WHAT!??" hollered Percy. "I need to eat!"

"I'll cook you up a lunch, don't worry," said Sergio. He rushed to the kitchen and made the only thing he really knew how to cook.

Percy looked at it with a frown. Then he sniffed it. "What's this?" he asked.

Sergio smiled nervously. "It's called *pizza*, sir. It's popular in Italy. Try it!"

So Percy tried it. He took one bite after another. Then he smiled!

"I love it! This will be the official food of Pirateville from now on!"

And that's how pizza came to Pieville.

FILL IN the missing information in this story plan.

Title: _____

The story takes place in <u>Pieville in the 1700s</u>. 1 _____

is a character in the story <u>who shoots down boats and kidnaps the sailors</u>.

2 _____ is another character in this story

who is a <u>sailor from Italy</u>. The first thing that happens in the story is that

3 _____

_____

A problem occurs when 4 _____.

The problem is solved when 5 _____.

The story ends with 6 _____.

READ the story.

Slam Dunk!

It was a hot summer day in New York City, and Graciela Cordez was stuck in her apartment. Graciela sat in the window and stared down the street.

"This stinks!" she sighed.

Then she saw a bunch of little creatures swarming through the streets from the river. Was it rats? Was it aliens?

"It's donuts!" cried Graciela.

Donuts of all kinds were rolling uphill from the donut factory. Then they attacked! Graciela watched as a hundred jelly-filled monsters swarmed over a girl on the corner and rolled her away. A giant gang of powdered donut holes surrounded the playground.

Graciela's father was a general in the army. She called him up and told him what was happening.

"Donuts, you say?" he said. "How can we fight donuts?"

"Listen!" said Graciela. "I know exactly what to do."

So an hour later, the army came. It had a big tanker truck that said "Coffee" in big green letters. The truck had a hose attached. The soldiers went down the city streets, spraying the donuts with coffee.

It worked! The donuts got dunked. Then everyone ate them.

Graciela got a medal from the President for her smart idea.

FILL IN the missing information in this story plan.

Title: _____

The story takes place 1_____.

2_____ is a character in the story who

3_____. <u>Graciela's father </u>is another

character in this story who 4_____.

The first thing that happens in the story is that

5_____.

A problem occurs when 6_____.

The problem is solved when 7_____.

The story ends with 8_____.

READ the story.

Babysitting Blues

Hugo was the happiest kid on Maple Street. His favorite band, the Charm Squad, was playing a free show in a park downtown on Saturday night. He couldn't wait to see them!

"You can't go," said his Mom.

"WHAT!?" cried Hugo. "Why not?"

"You have to baby-sit that night." She showed him the calendar. On Saturday night, it said, "Hugo baby-sits at Burstein's."

"Oh no!" moaned Hugo. "Not Baby Ben!"

Baby Ben Burstein was a total pain. He never stopped screaming, he never went to sleep, and he always barfed up his food.

Now Hugo was the saddest kid on Maple Street.

Then the phone rang. It was Baby Ben's mom. She called to ask Hugo if he could baby-sit Ben at his grandma's apartment downtown, because their house was being painted. Hugo said it was fine. But he was still sad.

Then Saturday night came, and Hugo saw where Baby Ben's grandma lived! Her apartment windows looked right over the park where they were setting up for the Charm Squad show. Hugo would have the best seat in the house! Best of all, Baby Ben liked the music too! He didn't barf the whole night.

FILL IN the story plan.

Title: _____

The story takes place 1_____.

2_____ is a character in the story

who 3_____.

4_____ is another character in this

story who is a <u>total pain to baby-sit</u>. The first thing that happens in the story is that

5_____.

A problem occurs when 6_____

_____.

The problem is solved when 7_____

_____.

The story ends with 8_____.

READ the story.

Down in the Basement

After her family moved in, Cassie hated the new apartment building right away.

"Where are all the kids?" she asked.

"Maybe they're at the playground," her mother said. She wanted Cassie to be happy. "Let's take a look."

But the kids in the playground were all too young.

"I guess there aren't any kids my age around here," Cassie sighed.

One day, Cassie's mother came up from the building's basement with a special smile.

"Would you like to help me wash some clothes?" she asked.

Cassie had nothing fun to do, so she went down to the laundry room with her mother. When they stepped out of the elevator into the basement, Cassie heard lots of shouting and laughter.

"What's that?" she asked.

"Why don't you check it out?" her mother said.

Cassie opened a door across from the laundry room and gasped. Inside the big room, a bunch of kids her age were playing games, jumping rope, and listening to music, while a few parents watched.

"Hi!" said a girl. "You must be the new kid. Want to pretend to be princesses locked in a tower?"

And that's how Cassie spent the afternoon.

FILL IN the story plan.

Title: _____

The story takes place 1_____.

2_____ is a character in the story

who 3_____.

4_____ is another character in the story

who 5_____.

The first thing that happens in the story is that 6_____

_____.

A problem occurs when 7_____

_____.

The problem is solved when 8_____

_____.

The story ends with 9_____

_____.

READ the story.

Robinson Family Vacation

Lionel couldn't believe they were really going to do it. His family planned to spend the entire summer sailing on the Pacific Ocean. His little sister Lucy was really excited, but Lionel thought it was the worst idea ever.

"Two months in a teeny-tiny boat?" he said. "With you guys?" Unlike the rest of his family, Lionel couldn't stand sailing. Plus, how would he get to play the video games he loved?

"It'll be great," said his father. "Total togetherness!"

"I hope we get stuck in a storm!" said Lucy.

"Can I bring my—?" started Lionel.

"No video games!" his mother broke in.

After two days in the boat, Lionel was ready to jump overboard. He was mad at his parents, he was sick of his sister, and he just wanted to be alone. But there was no room to be alone on the small sailboat.

Then a few days later, Lucy's wish for a storm came true. A dark cloud burst over their heads with pouring rain, lightning, and lots of wind. The storm flipped the Robinson's boat completely upside-down.

The radio on their boat wasn't working, so they couldn't call for help.

"All right!" yelled Mr. Robinson. "Let's get out."

"Out?" yelled Lionel. He couldn't believe his ears.

His mother made sure their life jackets were tight, and she turned on the little flashing lights called *beacons* that were attached to each jacket.

Lionel knew he had to be brave. He took his sister's hand, and together they climbed up out of the boat and into the ocean.

The rest of the storm was a blur. When Lionel opened his eyes, he found himself on a beach. He quickly looked around. His whole family was there! Lionel was so happy, he cried.

Nobody was hurt, but the island was very small, and there was no fresh water to drink. They couldn't stay there.

"We need to get this radio working," said Lionel's dad. He had put it in a watertight bag and kept it inside his life jacket. "I think it just needs batteries."

"But where will we get batteries?" asked Lucy.

Then Lionel pulled out his own watertight bag. Inside were his handheld video game player and his backup batteries. "What kind do you need?"

"Lionel! I said no video games!" snapped his mother.

But the rest of the family laughed.

They got the radio working and called the Coast Guard to come and take them home. Lionel spent the rest of the summer playing all the games he wanted.

Story Plan

FILL IN the story plan.

Title: _____

The story takes place 1 _____.

2 _____ is a character in the story

who 3 _____.

4 _____ are the other characters in this

story who 5 _____.

The first thing that happens is 6 _____.

A problem occurs when 7 _____.

After that, 8 _____

and 9 _____.

The problem is solved when 10 _____

_____.

The story ends with 11 _____

_____.

Compare & Contrast

PICK an article or story to read, and CHOOSE two subjects to compare and contrast. Then FILL OUT this worksheet.

The title is _____

I'm comparing and contrasting

subject 1, _____

with subject 2, _____

Details about subject 1

1. _____

2. _____

3. _____

4._____

5. _____

Details about subject 2

1. _____

2. _____

3. _____

4. _____

5. _____

For each detail ask yourself, is this detail something that belongs to only one of the subjects, or is it really something that is shared by both?

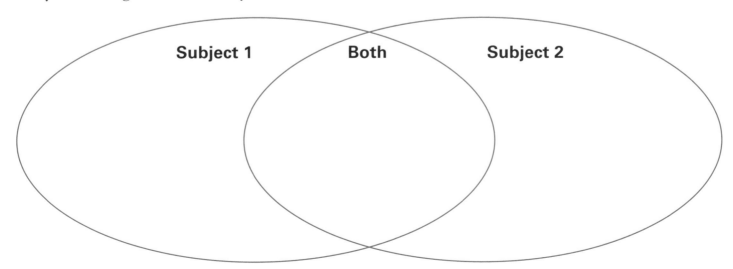

Compare & Contrast

PICK an article or story to read, and CHOOSE two subjects to compare and contrast. Then FILL OUT this worksheet.

The title is _____

I'm comparing and contrasting

subject 1, _____

with subject 2, _____

Details about subject 1

1. _____

2. _____

3. _____

4. _____

5. _____

Details about subject 2

1. _____

2. _____

3. _____

4. _____

5. _____

For each detail ask yourself, is this detail something that belongs to only one of the subjects, or is it really something that is shared by both?

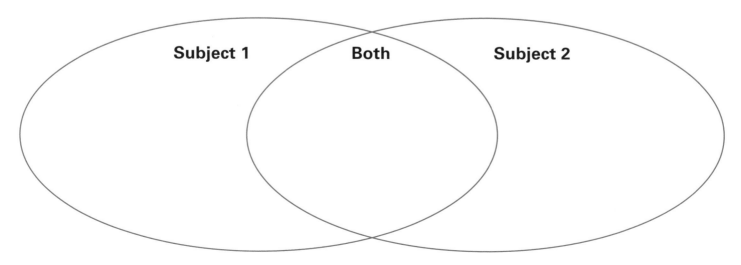

Subject 1   **Both**   **Subject 2**

Story Plan

PICK a story you've already read, then FILL OUT this worksheet.

Title _____

Main character _____

Character details _____

_____

The setting _____

_____

The first thing that happens is _____

_____

_____

The problem _____

_____

After that _____

_____

After that _____

_____

The solution _____

_____

_____

Story Plan

PICK a story you've already read, then FILL OUT this worksheet.

Title _____

Main character _____

Character details _____

_____

The setting _____

The first thing that happens is _____

_____

The problem _____

After that _____

After that _____

The solution _____

_____

_____

Stop & Go Story

Here's an article that will test all of your new talents!

READ the article, and FILL IN the blanks along the way.

 GO

All About SPIES!

Before you read, WRITE five questions you think this article will answer.

 STOP

1. _____

   _____

2. _____

   _____

3. _____

   _____

4. _____

   _____

5. _____

   _____

✓ Check It!

Page 105

Stop & Go Story

Suggestions:
- What tools do spies use?
- Do spies always wear disguises?
- Who are some famous spies?
- Why do we need spies?
- What kind of spies are there?

Page 106

Suggestions:
Know:
1. Spies find out secrets from other countries.
2. Spies use secret cameras and microphones to do their work.
3. Spying can be very dangerous.
4. Some spies are double agents.
5. James Bond is a famous fictional spy.

Learned:
1. Spies are called *intelligence agents*.
2. Spies use bugs and wiretaps.
3. Most countries have intelligence agencies.
4. Most new spies only have a high school diploma.
5. James Bond was based on a real spy named Dusko Popov.

Page 109

Yes:
- All the other countries are doing it.
- Spies can help catch enemy spies.
- During peacetime, spies can find a threat of terrorism or war.
- During wartime, spies can help the military.

No:
- Spying is very dangerous for the agents.
- We should trust other countries and use diplomacy instead.
- If an agent is caught, he may give up information or be turned.

Page 111

1. c
2. b
3. a
4. b
5. a

Page 112

Agent:
-Uses a disguise or cover
-Goes on missions
-Faces danger

Case Officer:
-Recruits the spy
-Uses own identity
-Sends spy on missions
-Uses the information collected
 by the spy

Both:
-Collect and deliver information
-Get training
-Risk discovery

Page 114

Main Idea 1: Types of Agents
Details: intelligence agents,
case officers, double agents

Main Idea 2: Tools of the Trade
Details: cameras, bugs, wiretaps,
five senses, codes, hiding places,
microdots, dead drops, code sheets,
maps, radio equipment

Main Idea 3: Why We Spy
Details: protect country, catch enemy
spies, help the military, prevent
terrorism

Main Idea 4: Reasons to Become a Spy
Details: money, love of country, thrills

Main Idea 5: Famous Spies
Details: James Bond, Dusko Popov,
Mata Hari, Yvonne Cormeau,
Aldrich Ames

STOP Now, FILL IN the What Do I Already Know? column.

What Do I Already Know?

What Did I Learn?

Now START READING the story.

Tools of the Spy Trade

Spies, also known as *intelligence agents*, have lots of tools to collect information secretly. (That's what intelligence is—information.) Agents might use a camera to photograph people, buildings, or documents. A *bug* can record conversations in a room, and a *wiretap* can record phone calls. An agent also uses his own five senses.

Spies also need to transmit information secretly. When an agent sends a message or report to his agency, the words need to be in code. The agency creates a *cipher*—like "A=1"—which tells the agent how to code his messages. If the cipher falls into enemy hands, those messages aren't safe!

Objects, like maps or photographs, need to be hidden (or *concealed*) inside everyday objects, like fake batteries, watches, or even hairbrushes! To be concealed, photographs can be shrunk down into a *microdot*, which looks like a tiny period on a sentence, but can contain an entire page of text when read through a microscope.

Once concealed, the spy might bring the information to a *dead drop*, a secret place prearranged between the agent and his bosses. The spy leaves the information at the drop in a brown paper bag or inside a fake rock. Then the boss comes by later to pick it up. This way, they're never seen together.

CONTINUE READING the story.

Why Spy?

Spying is dangerous work. Agents who are caught can be captured. And worse, a spy might give up his secrets when he's caught or even be turned into a double agent. Is it worth the risk?

Most, if not all, countries say "yes." Pretty much every country in the world has an intelligence agency. Countries need to spy to protect themselves. A whole branch of spying called *counterespionage* is devoted to catching enemy spies. And, of course, intelligence is really important during a war. A good spy can find information that can help a country win a key battle.

But what about during peacetime? If we have open relationships with other countries, we can use diplomats, like ambassadors, to find out information. We should trust each other!

In today's world, trust and intelligence go hand in hand. If there's a threat of terrorism or war that might hurt our country, we need to know about it. That's why we spy!

Q: Should countries spy on each other?

FILL IN the facts.

OPINION	FACTS
YES	_____
YES	_____
YES	_____
YES	_____
NO	_____
NO	_____
NO	_____
NO	_____

So? What do YOU think?

Should countries spy on each other?

Circle one: YES   NO

New Recruits

New spies are joining the ranks every day. Some people turn to spying for the money or because they're patriotic—they love their country, and they want to help protect it. And, of course, it can be an exciting job—some spies do it for the thrills!

Here's a little (fake) information about brand-new spies:

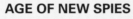

AGE OF NEW SPIES

GENDER OF NEW SPIES

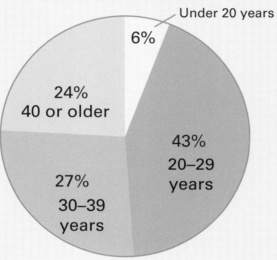

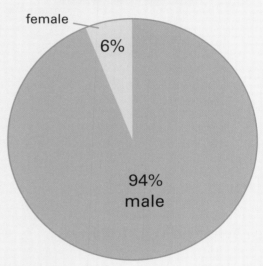

EDUCATION OF NEW SPIES

6%	No High School Diploma
42%	High School Diploma Only
20%	High School + Some College
20%	College Diploma
12%	College Diploma + More School

Note: A *diploma* is what you get when you graduate from a school.

STOP CHECK the right answers to each question!

1. How much education do most new spies have?

   - a. More than college
   - b. Less than high school
   - c. High School only

2. Are most new spies female?

   - a. Yes
   - b. No

3. How old are most new spies?

   - a. 20 to 29 years old
   - b. Under 20 years old
   - c. Over 40 years old

4. What percentage of new spies have more than a high school education?

   - a. 59%
   - b. 52%
   - c. 14%

5. Are most new spies 30 or older?

   - a. Yes
   - b. No

Stop & Go Story

CONTINUE READING the story, and FILL IN the blanks along the way.

GO

Types of Spies

Intelligence agents can't work alone. They are managed by a *case officer*. The case officer may even be the person who *recruited*, or hired, the spy. Both agents and case officers are working to collect and send information. And if they're discovered, that's a really bad thing. But the case officer doesn't do the actual spying. The case officer sends the spy on a mission, then takes and uses the information that the spy collects. While a spy may use a disguise or a cover story, the case officer never does. Agents and case officers get lots of training on how to collect and deliver information. But spies are the ones who really face danger!

STOP

Agent   **Both**   **Case Officer**

GO

Famous Spies

Everyone's heard of James Bond, or 007, the fictional British spy invented by author (and ex-spy) Ian Fleming. Bond was based on a real spy named Dusko Popov. Popov, codename "Tricycle," was a dashing businessman who fed lies to the Germans during World War II. (Sometimes misinformation can be useful too!)

Dancer Mata Hari is one of the most famous names in spying. But she wasn't really a very good spy during World War I. In the end, she was killed by a French firing squad.

Another female spy, Yvonne Cormeau, was much better. During World War II, Yvonne posed as "Annette," a child's nurse. Inside her purse, she hid code sheets, maps, and radio equipment. For over a year, she kept her cover story and sent coded messages to the Allies from inside enemy territory.

In 1994, an American named Aldrich Ames was caught working as a *double agent* in the CIA. A double agent is a spy who seems to work for one spy agency, while reporting information to the enemy agency. Aldrich and his wife were paid well by the Russians to spy on the CIA. After he was caught, Aldrich was sentenced to life in prison.

FILL IN the main ideas and details from this article.

Main Idea 1

_____

Details

_____

_____

_____

Main Idea 2

Tools of the Trade
_____

Details

_____

_____

_____

_____

_____

_____

Main Idea 3

_____

Details

_____

help the military
_____

_____

Main Idea 4

_____

Details

_____

_____

thrills
_____

Main Idea 5

_____

Details

_____

_____

Dusko Popv
_____

_____

What did you learn from this article? GO to page 106 and FILL IN the What Did I Learn? column.

Stop & Go Story

Let's review your skills with another story!

READ the story, and FILL IN the blanks along the way.

GO

Manolo's New Suit

Manolo was the vainest, smartest man in all the kingdom of Peronia. His castle was filled with closets and libraries. The closets were filled with suits. The libraries were filled with books. Manolo bought a new suit and a new book every week. His banker, the Lord High Banker, paid the bills with Manolo's gold.

One day, a new suit-maker came to town in a golden limo. She wore lots of bling. She even had a gold tooth! Manolo asked her to come to his castle right away.

When the suit-maker arrived, Manolo demanded that she make him a new suit.

"As a matter of fact, Your Majesty," she said. "I have an amazing new cloth that I've been eager to try out."

"Really?" cried Manolo. "What does it look like?"

"It's very special," she explained. "Only smart people can see this fabric. If you're not smart enough, the cloth will be invisible."

Manolo laughed. "Well, that might be a problem for some people, but I assure you, I'm super smart."

Turn the page for more.

✓ Check It!

Page 116-117

1. b: Because he lives in a castle, is called "Your Majesty," and sits on a throne.
2. b: Advisors were embarrassed, didn't praise the suit until they heard it could only be seen by smart people
3. Did you succeed in avoiding the words *naked* or *nude*?

Page 119

1. B: The Lord High Banker, the Lord High Advisor, the Lord High Librarian, the Lord High Tennis Coach, the Lord High Suit Inspector.
2. A: Dmitri.
3. C: Write your own opinion.
4. D: Because they're afraid the king will think they're not smart.

Page 120

Title: Manolo's New Suit
1. in the kingdom of Peronia
2. Manolo
3. is a very smart, vain king
4. Dmitri
5. wants to be a suit-maker when he grows up
6. the king gets a new suit that doesn't exist
7. he goes on parade to show his new suit to the people
8. tells them if they don't see it, they must be stupid
9. Dmitri tells the king the truth
10. King Manolo making Dmitri his Lord High Suit Inspector

CONTINUE READING the story, and FILL IN the blanks along the way.

So the suit-maker measured Manolo carefully, then went home to make the suit. When she came back a few days later, she had a big box.

Manolo was meeting with his advisors, but he jumped up from his throne to try on his new suit. When he came back into the room, his advisors gasped. One of them turned bright red. Two of them looked away.

"Y-your M-Majesty!" the Lord High Advisor, said. "You're n–!"

"It fits like a glove!" cried the suit-maker. "It just needs a little more work." She stepped up to Manolo with a needle and made a few stitches. "There!"

Manolo laughed. "You see, my friends, only intelligent people like ourselves can see this wonderful fabric. If you were stupid, you'd think I was standing here naked!"

The advisors looked at each other. They were supposed to be very smart.

One by one they smiled. "What a terrific suit! Very stylish!" they cried.

Now, CHECK the right answers, and FILL IN the blanks!

1. Who is Manolo?

☐ a. A rich suit-maker

☐ b. The king of Peronia

☐ c. A wealthy businessman

How do you know? _____

2. Can the advisors see the special fabric?

☐ a. Yes

☐ b. No

How do you know? _____

_____

_____

GO

 Just then, the king's wife and teenage son came into the room. When the queen saw Manolo, she fell to the ground in a faint. Her ladies-in-waiting giggled and blushed and tried to wake her up.

Finally she lifted her head. "Manolo," she said, "what's going on?"

"It's my new suit, dearest," said Manolo. "Don't you like it?"

The Lord High Librarian added: "Only smart people can see the fabric, you know."

STOP

Now it's YOUR turn!

WRITE the rest of the conversation between Manolo and his family. Don't forget, they won't admit that he's naked. So don't use the words *naked* or *nude*.

_____

_____

_____

_____

_____

Turn the page for more.

GO

Manolo liked his new suit so much that he decided to wear it in a New Suit Parade. The people of Peronia couldn't wait to see it. Everyone was talking about the special fabric.

"But there's no such thing as invisible cloth," said Dmitri, the butcher's son. He knew all about fabric. He wanted to be a suit-maker to the king when he grew up.

His father ruffled Dmitri's hair. "I'm sure you'll see it, Dmitri. You're very smart."

"He's the smartest boy in school," said his mother proudly.

On the day of the parade, Dmitri made sure to get a front row seat. The king and his advisors came down the street led by the Lord High Tennis Coach. The crowd cheered at first, then got quiet.

"Well?" cried the king. "What do you think?" He walked up to Dmitri's family and stood in front of them.

Dmitri's Uncle Steve said it was the nicest suit he'd ever seen. Dmitri's cousin Jessie said it looked very warm. Then the king turned to Dmitri.

Dmitri smiled. "Either I'm dumb or you are," he said, "because you sure look naked to me."

King Manolo frowned. "I'm sorry to hear that," he said. "I guess you're not as smart as you look."

Dmitri's father spoke up. "Oh yeah? Then I'm stupid too because I can see your outtie bellybutton!"

And Dmitri's mother, "You've got freckles on your bottom!"

Suddenly the whole town was talking about the naked king. And they weren't saying nice things. They were shocked when Manolo laughed and patted Dmitri on the back. "I hope you all learned your lesson," the king said. "It's always better to be honest than smart. Somebody bring me a robe!"

That day, the king made Dmitri his Lord High Suit Inspector.

STOP

MARK each question with an A, B, C, or D in the box.

Then ANSWER the questions.

A = Right There Question   *B = Think & Search Question*

C = On Your Own Question   *D = Author and Me Question*

1. Who are the king's advisors?

    ☐ _____

2. Who finally tells the king the truth?

    ☐ _____

3. If you were a king, would you rather buy books or suits?

    ☐ _____

4. Why does everyone lie about seeing the fabric?

    ☐ _____

FILL IN the story plan for this big story.

Title:_____

The story takes place 1_____

2_____ is a character in the story who

3_____.

4_____ is another character in this story who

5_____.

A problem occurs when 6_____.

After that, 7_____ and

8_____.

The problem is solved when 9_____.

The story ends with 10_____

_____.